RAMSAY MACDONALD

A Labour Tragedy?

PERSONALITIES *and* POWERS

RAMSAY MACDONALD

A Labour Tragedy?

Duncan Watts

Hodder & Stoughton

A MEMBER OF THE HODDER HEADLINE GROUP

Acknowledgements

The front cover shows Ramsay MacDonald reproduced courtesy of The Keystone Collection, London.

The publishers would like to thank the following for their permission to reproduce material in this volume:

Addison Wesley Longman for an extract from *The Rise and Fall of the Labour Party, 1880–1945* by P. Adelman; The Observer © for an extract from an article by J. L. Garvin in *The Observer* August 1921.

The publishers would like to thank the following for their permission to reproduce illustrations in this volume:

Hulton Getty p. 62, p. 124; The National Museum of Labour, Manchester p. 86, p. 122; Punch Publications p. 77, p. 98.

Every effort has been made to trace and acknowledge ownership of copyright. The publishers will be glad to make suitable arrangements with any copyright holder whom it has not been possible to contact.

Order queries: please contact Bookpoint Ltd, 39 Milton Park, Abingdon, Oxon OX14 4TD. Telephone: (44) 01235 400414, Fax: (44) 01235 400454. Lines are open from 9.00–6.00, Monday to Saturday, with a 24 hour message answering service. Email address: orders@bookpoint.co.uk

British Library Cataloguing in Publication Data
A catalogue record for this title is available from The British Library

ISBN 0 340 697 44X

First published 1998
Impression number 10 9 8 7 6 5 4 3 2 1
Year   2002 2001 2000 1999 1998

Copyright © 1998 Duncan Watts

Typeset by Fakenham Photosetting Ltd, Fakenham, Norfolk
Printed in Great Britain for Hodder & Stoughton Educational, a division of Hodder Headline Plc, 338 Euston Road, London NW1 3BH by Redwood Books, Trowbridge, Wilts.

CONTENTS

INTRODUCTION

The personality and leadership of James Ramsay MacDonald have left an indelible mark on the history of the Labour Party. For many years after his passing from the political scene, he was regarded as the man who betrayed his colleagues both within and outside the House of Commons, and some of his critics displayed intense personal venom both towards him and his legacy.

Evidence of his position in the demonology of the Labour Movement still surfaces from time to time even more than a half century after his death. In 1976, at a time when cuts in government expenditure were under consideration, Tony Benn circulated the Cabinet minutes of August 1931 among his ministerial colleagues, some of whom were deeply affronted. For any prominent figure to be accused of 'MacDonaldism' was too heavy a political cross to bear. Even today, right-wing Labour members who allow themselves to become too isolated from party orthodoxy still run the risk of being charged with behaviour akin to that of Labour's first Prime Minister. Those supposedly on the left are not immune from being tainted with such connections. In the Miners' Strike of 1984–5, the new leader, Neil Kinnock, was placed in a difficult position and felt unable to support the coalminers outright for fear of the damage such an endorsement might have done to Labour's national reputation. Because of his ambivalence on the issue, he was dubbed Ramsay MacKinnock on more than one banner hoisted by outraged trade unionists.

When MacDonald died, there was little mourning beyond that of his immediate family and circle of personal friends. His reputation stands higher today, but he is not viewed as a figure of particular interest, nor as one to be much admired. For some members of the Labour Party, he remains a traitor; to others who are less bitter, he remains a mediocrity. If he is an embarrassment to Labour, he earns little praise from outside the party. 'Progressives' of whatever political hue tend to lament his failure to exhibit bold economic thinking at the time of the Great Depression, and to make adverse comparisons with the way in which President Franklin Roosevelt inspired the American nation with his promise of 'action now' in the New Deal programme. Conservatives have displayed little sympathy for the man who put himself at their helm in the National Government of 1931. MacDonald remains unlamented and by some despised.

Of course, for many years it was fashionable for historians to criticise the quality of all leadership in Britain between the wars, and Professor Mowat's description of the era as 'the rule of the pygmies' has been deeply etched into the national memory. It is true that the political giants were out of fashion (Lloyd George ignored and Churchill in the wilderness), and that the men who led the nation lacked the vision and effectiveness of some of their opponents and rivals. But it would be wrong to assume that, because the giants were out, the lesser men in charge of the conduct of affairs were totally unfitted for the premiership. The comments of Churchill on his colleagues and opponents were singularly pungent, and his description of MacDonald as a 'boneless wonder' so grossly overstated the attack which could be made that it deserves to be cast aside for a more balanced judgement.

The leadership of the inter-war premiers was not noticeably inferior to that provided by Asquith before the First World War, or by a succession of prime ministers since 1945. The trouble was that the challenges of the decades before the Second World War were particularly serious ones, unemployment and the rise of the dictators. MacDonald was more concerned with the first than the second, and the failure to grapple successfully with the spectre of 'life on the dole' was a blight upon his record from a national point of view. From a party point of view, that alone was disappointing enough. But the decision taken in August 1931 to forsake his party and lead a Conservative-dominated coalition was considerably more disconcerting, and it is this abandonment which provoked the charges so often made against him.

Labour supporters, then and now, find it hard to see how the man who came from nowhere (the most lowly person to make it to the top in British politics) and who wrote and spoke so effectively on their behalf, who went on to make a principled stand against British involvement in the First World War and was prepared to take the flak of being branded as dishonourable and lacking in patriotism, could allow himself to become the prisoner of his political opponents – even worse, one who headed an administration which fought an election against his old party and helped to inflict a bruising defeat upon it. But before we can explore many of the issues raised by his important career in Labour politics, we need to examine the early history of the party in Britain so that we have a background context into which we can place his life in sharper focus.

THE RISE OF THE LABOUR PARTY IN BRITAIN

The extension of the vote to working people in 1867 and 1884 made it necessary for the established parties to put forward attractive policies to appeal to them. If the Conservative and Liberal parties had proved capable of producing social reforms, on a wide scale, to benefit the new voters then maybe a specifically working man's party would have been unnecessary. Although the Conservatives under Disraeli (1874–80) did briefly tackle some social topics, such as the rights of unions and the hours of workers, the party was basically an upper-class one uninterested in popular reform, and by the end of the century it offered even less prospect of social improvement. The Liberals, the more progressive party, did have a radical wing, but the party contained various groups, such as the Whigs and some manufacturers, who did not favour change. Moreover, Gladstone, the leader for several years after 1880, was too immersed in Irish affairs to take up the 'condition of the people' question. Local Liberal associations were often unwilling to open their membership to working people, and were even more reluctant to choose them as parliamentary candidates. Thus, because neither main party could adapt sufficiently, a new party became more likely and in the late nineteenth century various moves were made to bring about its formation.

EARLY MOVES: THE APPEARANCE OF SOCIALIST DOCTRINES

In 1869 a Labour Representation League was formed to get working men into the House of Commons, but it was short-lived. In 1874, two working men did get elected as Liberals. It was in the 1880s, however, that there was a growing interest in the new socialist doctrines associated with Karl Marx and Frederick Engels, two Germans then living in Britain. Marx died in 1883, but his influence was to be felt for many years. He argued that private ownership ('of the means of production, distribution and exchange') or capitalism was the root cause of the plight of the working class. Greedy, profit-seeking employers exploited their workers by paying low wages and making them work long hours – to enrich their own pockets. Thus socialists argued for public ownership or nationalisation of industry, and believed this would bring about a better economic system. They wanted greater equality, a fairer distribution of wealth and to replace competition by greater cooperation. At first these new ideas had a limited circulation, mainly among middle-class writers and thinkers, though some trade union leaders were strong Marxists. In the Great Depression of the late nineteenth century, when Britain's agricultural and industrial performance was under increased challenge from abroad, some people were attracted to socialist ideas, seeing a more 'planned' economy as preferable to one prone to a recurring cycle of booms and slumps, and thus a way out of Britain's difficulties. Marx believed that the working class (proletariat) should use any means available – strikes, violence, even civil war – to throw off their backs those who oppressed and exploited them. But in England the socialist movement generally favoured peaceful means to bring about their aims. The differing strands of their thinking and general approach are seen in the note on **Early Socialism and British Socialist Societies.**

a note on . . .

EARLY SOCIALISM AND BRITISH SOCIALIST SOCIETIES

Modern socialism began with the so-called Utopians in the first half of the nineteenth century. In their propaganda they wrote of an ideal form of society, to be achieved not by revolution but by peaceful means. Some, such as Robert Owen, established model communities which would provide examples of a new and better way of life.

This form of socialism was rejected by Karl Marx and Frederick Engels, whose early views were set out in the *Communist Manifesto* they jointly produced in 1848. They had little sympathy with the attempt to realise a socialist utopia through appeals to humanity and morality, and instead proclaimed their belief in the class struggle. Organisation of the proletariat (the exploited workers) on a class basis and subsequent revolution was their preferred approach, and they saw the ultimate triumph of the proletariat as an inevitable process. They used the term 'scientific socialism' to distinguish their variety from the utopian form. Organised socialist parties which described themselves as 'Marxist' developed in Germany, and elsewhere in countries such as Austria, Britain, France and Russia, in the last decades of the century – although Marx had died (1883) by the time many of them were proclaiming his theories.

Most socialist parties joined the Second International when it was established in 1889. Although it was looked upon as the centre of world revolution, there was a permanent struggle between those who revised Marxist theory by suggesting that socialism might be achieved by gradual reform and peaceful evolution (revisionists), and those who insisted on the purity of Marx's approach and believed in forceful revolution.

In Britain, socialism developed along evolutionary lines, and there were not many advocates of the more revolutionary form. There were relatively few people who could be described as socialists by any modern definition, although in the closing decades of the century the term was often used very loosely in Britain to describe anyone who believed in using the power of the state to modify the excesses of capitalism for the benefit the mass of the people.

Of the avowedly socialist societies, four are worthy of mention:

The Social Democratic Federation (SDF) was led by a Marxist Henry Hyndman, a dictatorial stockbroker who had once been a Tory radical. Throughout his life he continued to address his audiences in a frockcoat and top hat, but he had been converted to Marxism after reading *Das Kapital*. It was largely because of a dislike of his autocratic approach that a breakaway group was formed, the Socialist League. The SDF continued to advocate a militant programme – involving, among other things, abolition of armies, of indirect taxation and of the monarchy – into the new century.

The Socialist League was led by the poet and craftsman William Morris, who split from the SDF in 1885. No Marxist, Morris wanted a fairer society in which 'the means of the production of wealth must be declared and treated as the common property of all'.

The Fabian Society, founded in 1884, most clearly pointed the way forward by stressing the idea of letting socialist ideas gradually permeate the other parties. It took its name from the Roman general Quintus Fabius Maximus who was renowned as a military leader for his avoidance of pitched battles and his preference for using more insidious raiding parties which would chip away at the enemy. The Society was composed largely of intellectuals and writers such as the Webbs, George Bernard Shaw, H. G. Wells and others who in numerous pamphlets stressed the idea of 'gradualism'. Sidney Webb spoke of 'the inevitability of gradualness' (an indication that socialism could only be achieved by democratic means and not by sudden or violent change). Members tended to be more idealistic than the more materialistic Marxist continental socialists, and they stressed the need to spread their conviction that socialism was a better system than capitalism, rather than operate through the class struggle. The Fabian approach was to have a profound impact on the development of the Labour Party as a party of moderate reform.

The Independent Labour Party (ILP) was founded by Keir Hardie in Bradford (1893). The ILP comprised mainly provincial intellectuals who were suspicious of London middle-class socialists. It was created in the north because already several short-lived working-class socialist bodies had been established on both sides of the Pennines to protest about dire living conditions and in particular low wages. The new creation was intended to be a nationwide organisation dedicated to the establishment of a working-class voice in Parliament. Many present in Bradford were socialists, but the choice of name indicated the importance attached to securing broader labour support – both for the additional membership and access to union funds that this might bring.

Meanwhile, at a time when socialist ideas were arousing more interest, there was a new development within the trade union movement. Older skilled trade unions and their leaders had been happy to work through traditional political channels, and many were loosely aligned with the Liberal Party. Younger men, especially those in unskilled unions, were less willing to share the assumptions which employers and trade unionists had long taken for granted about such things as the laws of supply and demand, and they began to doubt the theory as well as the practice of capitalism. Unskilled workers were organising more effectively and becoming increasingly militant. A more robust consciousness of working-class solidarity strengthened the aggressive tendencies of the new unions and the new leadership. Fearing cuts in their wages and unemployment, and unhappy at their grim conditions, such workers joined the 'New Unions'. The New Unionism movement fought hard against the employers: two notable successes were the Matchgirls' Strike in 1888 at Bryant & May's Company and, particularly, the London Dock Strike of 1889, led by three socialists, Tillett, Burns and Mann. These were successful strikes, but many others failed, and the legal position of unions was also insecure. So many working people realised that they needed representation in Parliament if anti-union legislation was to be repealed and if their rights were to be respected. Working-class MPs could press for such improvements.

Faith in the Liberal Party as their best vehicle for progress had ebbed away, and many trade unionists no longer believed that the party could adequately represent working-class interests. Some men, such as Keir Hardie and Ramsay MacDonald, had tried to work through the party, only to find themselves distrusted and rejected by their local associations, and they came to realise that they were being exploited as allies without being accepted as equals. In 1892, Hardie, a Scottish miner, was elected as MP for West Ham. He was not a Lib-Lab, but rather a genuine socialist working man. He wanted to see an independent group of labour men in the House of Commons and, without TUC support, he campaigned for the creation of a new body, the Independent Labour Party (ILP), which was set up in Bradford in 1893. This seemed to be a way by which the aspirations of working men could be expressed in action, yet it was soon apparent that the working-class movement was weak and relatively impotent. The new body was not immediately successful in the 1895 election, and Hardie saw the need to get union funds and support if the party were to succeed. By the end of the nineteenth century, several union leaders were ready to listen to socialists when they argued that there must a separate party to protect the interests of labour. If the activities of middle-class socialists and working-class leaders were allowed to remain so diversified, then there was little chance that the working-class movement could make much headway. If they pooled their resources and concerted their efforts in one organisation, then they might bring about a change in the structure of politics and alter the whole climate of political debate.

THE FORMATION OF THE LABOUR REPRESENTATION COMMITTEE (LRC)

In January 1900, at a meeting in London, 116 men from 65 unions, the Social Democratic Federation (SDF), the Fabians and the ILP met together and quickly agreed to set up a Labour Representation Committee to work for the election of a separate group of working-class MPs in the House of Commons. Two LRC members were successful in the general election of that year, one being Hardie, MP for Merthyr Tydfil. Outside Parliament, the secretary of the new organisation, Ramsay MacDonald, worked hard to build up support among the unions for their money was still needed. It was this body, the LRC, which followed up its success in the 1906 election by undergoing a change of name. It became an official party, renaming itself the Labour Party.

MacDonald became the chairman of the Labour Party in 1911, he resigned in 1914 because of his opposition to British participation in the First World War. Yet although the war was to be a difficult time for MacDonald, it was in some respects helpful to the Labour Party. Some of its leaders gained ministerial experience for the first time, and the Liberal Party suffered a damaging personal split between the supporters of Asquith and Lloyd George which seriously undermined its strength. When the fighting was over the former Liberal Chancellor, Lloyd George, remained as Prime Minister of a predominantly Conservative Coalition, and the Labour Party benefited from a rapid Liberal decline. Wartime divisions over the war, political as well as personal, had undermined the belief of many progressive people in the Liberal Party as the best means of achieving peace and reform, and in particular the newly enfranchised working men (and some women) who began to vote in 1918 looked for a new political home.

MacDonald assumed the leadership of the Labour Party in 1922 (the first time that there was a leader, as opposed to a chairman of the PLP), and it was his achievement to take the party into government in 1924 and again in 1929, albeit on a minority basis. That Labour should have gone from being a third party in 1914 to a governing one a decade later was in no small measure due to MacDonald's efforts before and after the war. His services to the party were apparent to all within the Labour Movement. Then came the debacle. In the midst of the depression and an ever-worsening financial crisis in August 1931, he agreed to lead a national government which included Conservatives and Liberals. Although three other Labour ministers were willing to serve under him, most of the party were thoroughly disillusioned. When he campaigned against his old party in the election of October 1931 to seek public backing, many of his former colleagues thought he was a traitor and shortly afterwards they expelled him.

The party which MacDonald did so much to create and place on a secure footing in the early days was seriously weakened in 1931, and but for the war might have been out of office for a generation or more. The scale of the damage done by his handling of events was deeply serious and left the party dazed and in a sense of shock. Those who had known the MacDonald of an earlier era could barely understand what had happened. The general secretary of the party, Jim Middleton, wrote to him on 27 August 1931, and his letter expresses the confusion of a close associate who was baffled by what had come to pass:

> I am too full and puzzled to write at length. There is much, I feel, that is 'greatly dark' . . . on the merits of the situation, like practically everyone of your political friends, I feel strongly and instinctively unconvinced. As to your own stand – one simply witnesses it with the awe the heroic is bound to command, mingled with almost the deepest sadness I have ever known . . . Amid all the . . . unhappinesses of these last days – those much unhappier days of twenty years ago return . . . to my mind.

Others were less kindly, and it was not long before the charges levelled at MacDonald became much more serious. It was not a matter of his having merely made a misjudgement. The suggestion was made that he had deliberately done his best to 'smash' the party which he had helped to build. In Sidney Webb's version of the Plot Theory, the idea of a national (coalition) government seemed 'to have been germinating in the Prime Minister's mind for months before the blow was struck'. He referred to the 'drama' which MacDonald had himself 'staged'. As Lord Simon, a National Liberal colleague in that administration later wrote: 'The denunciations heaped upon MacDonald's head by many who had previously idolised him were the most violent I have ever known in British politics.'

HISTORIANS AND RAMSAY MACDONALD

MacDonald's character and reputation, so often slighted since 1931, were once admired by those who knew and wrote about him. They recognised that his combination of qualities enabled him to stand head and shoulders above his party contemporaries. No one could match him in the area of administrative and organisational expertise, or in his parliamentary exposition. Not for nothing did Emmanuel Shinwell, once a young associate but later a convinced opponent, describe the MacDonald of the early 1920s as 'a prince among men'.

Many of the subsequent judgements on MacDonald are inevitably much affected by the view taken by the writer of what happened in 1931, although there are earlier studies which throw some light upon his personality. Herbert Tracey's *The Rt. Hon. J. Ramsay MacDonald: A Biographical Study* (1924) presented a flattering picture of his value and potential as leader of the party of the working class. Hessell Tiltman wrote *James Ramsay MacDonald: Labour's Man of Greatness* in 1929, and again portrayed him as a man of the future, ideally equipped to lead the party. Mary Agnes Hamilton produced *J. Ramsay MacDonald* in 1929, an updated version of two earlier works which contain helpful insights into his character from one who moved in the 1920s from being a loyal devotee to a more critical – if still well-disposed – observer.

After 1931, the emphasis of the literature on MacDonald changed, and several hostile articles began to appear by Sidney Webb, Harold Laski and others active in the Labour Movement. Autobiographies such as Snowden's in 1934 and (much later) Shinwell's offer hostile insights. However, for a lengthy study, it was MacNeill Weir who wrote the long *Tragedy of Ramsay MacDonald: A Political Biography* (1938) to which the near contemporary could turn. He had served under the Prime Minister in a junior capacity, and was not unsympathetic to his dilemma in the midst of the dramatic events of 1931. However, the overall tone of the book then underway but finished a few years later is sharply condemnatory, and sees MacDonald as the author and key player in the crisis which owed much to his ambition and love of office.

The official biography, *Ramsay MacDonald*, finally appeared in 1977, written by David Marquand, an academic whose political stance was that of a social democrat. It is a thorough (903-page!) examination of the life of MacDonald which is based upon an exhaustive reading of the papers, and comes up with a more sympathetic study than had previously been available. It is critical in parts, not least of the handling of events in 1931, but overall it rehabilitated the reputation of a man long viewed with disdain and, in some cases, derision.

Finally, Austin Morgan wrote *J. Ramsay MacDonald* in the 'Lives of the Left' series, in 1987. This is written from the standpoint of an independent socialist who is a self-confessed Marxist. Yet despite his immersion in, and commitment to, left-wing politics, the writer has attempted to portray the contribution made by MacDonald in his earlier life to the evolution of British socialism and to the Labour Party, whilst having grave reservations about the turn taken by his career in the 1930s. He sees the decision in 1931 to lead a coalition government as 'totally unnecessary' and dwells upon the damage done to Labour by such an action.

The time is ripe for a reassessment in the light of the writings available, and in this portrait there is greater coverage of the private world of MacDonald than that given in the Morgan study, although primarily this is a political account. There are certainly many questions to be answered about Ramsay MacDonald, the man and the politician, and it is the purpose of this short volume to attempt to provide an answer to some of them. It is not a defence or a vindication of his performance as leader and Prime Minister, more an attempt to understand him better. It is intended to place the man and his leadership in the context of the evolution of the Labour Party, and to assess the scale of his contribution to the Labour Movement and to the nation at large.

timeline		
	1866	born of poor parents in Lossiemouth
	1893	joins Independent Labour Party
	1900	becomes first secretary of LRC
	1906	becomes an MP
	1911–14	chairman of Labour Party
	1914	opposes British involvement in World War
	1918	loses parliamentary seat
	1922	becomes MP; chosen as first Labour leader
	1924	becomes first Labour Prime Minister
	1929–31	serves as Prime Minister for second time
	1931	forms National Government
	1935	resigns as Prime Minister; serves as Lord President under Baldwin
	1937	dies on voyage to South America.

2

MACDONALD'S EARLY LIFE AND WORK TO 1914

James Ramsay MacDonald was born of poor parents in the Scottish village of Lossiemouth, a small fishing village on the coast of Morayshire, in October 1866. His father was John MacDonald, his mother Anne Ramsay. They did not live together, and James was illegitimate. He was christened James McDonald Ramsay, but in school he was known as J. Macdonald – Jamie to his friends. At home he was called Ramsay, but it was to be several years before the name evolved into its later form, James Ramsay MacDonald.

His father soon disappeared from the scene and the young boy only ever saw him once. His mother worked as a fisherwoman and in the fields, whilst doing dressmaking in her spare time as a way of making extra money. He was brought up by his mother as the only child living at his grandmother's home, in what MacNeill Weir called 'grinding but not hopeless poverty'. Several children in the area were brought up in single parent families and the local kirk could accept the situation the more easily as the parents had not been living together 'in sin', yet nonetheless there was much disapproval from respectable folk within the family and in the neighbourhood. Jamie was conscious of hostility towards himself and his mother, and later described it as a cause of much hurt and resentment to him. He found his status difficult to accept, and although the matter of his origins did not surface in his public life until mentioned by an opponent in 1915, it troubled him in those early years.

In 1896 he still felt that 'all my early memories are wretched to me', and his difficulty in gaining acceptance in his view accounted for his fiery temper: 'As far back as I can remember, I had a grudge against the world rankling in me.' Yet he did well in the parish school he attended – his high spirits and tendency to play truant notwithstanding – and received a solid education. He left at 14, but after a summer of farm-work he received a fortunate opportunity. There was a vacancy at his school for a pupil-teacher, and he returned to take it up and by so doing was able to make rapid intellectual progress over the next four years.

He was interested in learning, and his particular enthusiasms were science and literature. He liked political and social discussion and joined the local debating society, becoming its secretary. He was combative in debate, his serious and argumentative nature making him an effective speaker. As an agrarian radical, he acquired a local reputation for his disapproval of aristocratic privilege.

MacDonald was by his late teens a tall, handsome young man with a soft Scottish accent who was looking for wider horizons. He possessed a driving ambition and wanted to achieve something, yet he was beset by inner doubts and anxieties and wondered if he would make anything of himself. A decade or so later, he could still say that 'something is constantly saying to me that I will do nothing myself, but that I will enable someone else to do something'.

He left home to move to Bristol in mid-1885, and there he worked in a newly-organised Boys' and Young Men's Guild run by a clergyman at St Stephen's Church. Social work was his chosen career for the present, but it was socialism that became his vocation for it was in Bristol that he came into contact with emergent socialist ideas. He became a member of the small group known as the Social Democratic Federation (SDF). He soon established himself, and within a very short time was lecturing fellow-members, organising a library and addressing the public in the open air. Yet his appointment at St Stephen's was short-lived, and he returned to Lossiemouth later that year. His intention to found a local branch of the SDF did not materialise, for he became disenchanted with its intolerance and sectarianism, and with the domineering leadership of its Marxist leader, Henry Hyndman. He flirted with forming a splinter group, and promoted his ideas on so doing in the *Christian Socialist*. The resulting Socialist Union of Young Men had a short lifespan, as did the paper, but the involvement illustrates the young activist's early commitment to a combination of Christian and socialist thinking.

He moved to London in 1886, where he was unemployed for some time. He had arrived in the middle of a trade depression, and in between his often fruitless searches for work he could only afford to sustain himself by eating oatmeal (sent from home) and drinking warm water. Intermittently, he supported himself through a variety of clerical jobs. They were not well paid, and for much of the time he continued to live in poverty.

EARLY POLITICAL CAREER

Shortly after his arrival in London he joined the Fabian Society; he was soon an active member and was later to serve on its executive from 1894 to 1900. Members were impressed by his grasp of their ideas, and he admired their unsentimental and practical approach. He was also active on the streets, taking part in the notorious Bloody Sunday of 1889 when police and troops clashed with demonstrators over the demand of the unskilled dockworkers for 6d an hour pay. He saw himself as a firm defender of the right of free speech, and was willing to declare his stance in public.

He was encouraged to find that there was a strong Scottish input in London meetings of assorted groups on the left. He was by the mid-1880s an active socialist and noted with pleasure that 'the spirit of socialism is abroad, not only stirring the lower ranks of labour to discontent, but moving those whose physical wants are all provided for'. Political involvement was, however, only one aspect of his life. It was matched by a desire for self-improvement. He was determined to make something of his career, and saw learning as the key. He began to read and study profusely. Naturally industrious, he attended a variety of evening classes, with a view to obtaining a scholarship from South Kensington Museum.

It was through the Fabian connection that he met Thomas Lough, a 'Liberal and Radical' candidate for West Islington, a man of comfortable means who was also a loyal supporter of the Liberal leader, Gladstone. MacDonald served as his private secretary for the next four years, and was on the one hand involved in metropolitan Liberalism whilst on the other increasingly mingling with more radical figures in the local party. His experience was valuable for he gained an insight into the mechanics of party politics, and a chance to witness a higher stratum of society which he was subsequently to find increasingly attractive.

In the same era he revealed a passing interest in Scottish devolution, and became the London secretary of the Scottish Home Rule Association. In this capacity he first met Keir Hardie, and when Hardie stood as a Labour and Home Rule parliamentary candidate for the first time he wrote to wish him well. But MacDonald still saw himself as a Liberal, believing that the party and the creed could be 'reconstructed' to allow more scope for more 'advanced' people such as himself who saw much merit in socialist thinking.

In each of his early roles he soon displayed obvious talent, and even generally unsympathetic writers such as Weir commented that 'no sooner had he joined any organisation than he was lifted almost at once into an executive position'. The Fabians saw him as a useful link with Liberalism, for he was just the man to 'permeate' the established party with their much newer ideas. He continued to give lectures in Fabian philosophy, and developed his own programme for a just society. He wrote a pamphlet in 1892, *The New Charter*, setting out his political credo – he argued for land nationalisation and social reform, taking up such issues as an eight-hour day for workers and measures to tackle poverty. He also involved himself in the Fellowship of New Life, an ethical society which espoused cooperative notions. Led by a Scotsman, it aimed to develop 'the cultivation of a perfect character in each and all'. MacDonald was attracted to such an idea, for he recognised that if it was the case that socialism would prove to be morally superior to capitalism then it was necessary that there should be a mass of people in society who in their outlook and behaviour were moved by the highest ideals. Again, he quickly became the secretary of the Fellowship, whose thinking he so much much admired.

Yet his active life, with its blend of writing, speaking and organising still did not bring him significant personal happiness. His political life had not taken off in the way that he hoped it might. He did not personally get the opportunity to stand for Parliament, for in 1894 he failed to be adopted as a Lib-Lab candidate at Southampton after the old guard fought a strong campaign to keep out the working-class intruder. A little later that year, the local Liberal Party in a Sheffield division did not adopt a trade unionist for an important by-election, and MacDonald supported a rival candidate.

MacDonald was a socialist on the left of the Liberal Party, but he was becoming disillusioned with the Liberals for they were clearly not committed to achieving fundamental social change of the sort he favoured. As he told Hardie: 'I have stuck to the Liberals up to now, hoping that they might do something to justify the trust that we have put in them.' The Southampton and by-election episodes convinced him that 'it was quite impossible . . . to maintain my position as a Liberal any longer'. By July 1894, he had joined the Independent Labour Party formed by Hardie the previous year. As he told the leader, 'Liberalism, and more particularly Liberal associations, have definitely declared against Labour.' He now saw himself as an exponent of Labourism, a word much used by ILP members in their first annual conference. He had finally broken with Liberalism as his personal faith, for he believed that it had failed the working class. However, as with some others who shared his outlook, he often mingled in circles in which left-wing Liberals operated.

In the 1895 general election he stood as the Independent Labour Party candidate in Southampton but polled only 867 votes; none of the other 27 ILP candidates was victorious elsewhere. But in the following year he served on the National Administrative Council of the organisation, and along with Hardie, Philip Snowden (a rousing socialist lecturer) and others he became a prominent spokesman. He was seen by other members at this time as one of the more right-wing among them. Within the Fabian Society, the reverse was true and he tended to criticise its approach and policies from a left perspective. He would have liked to see an agreement between the two bodies so that they did not oppose each other in local elections. To this effect, he organised a meeting in his house of the leading spokesmen for each organisation, but no deal was done. He also wanted to see some Fabian funds used to help develop the research and propaganda side of the ILP. The Webbs were not sympathetic to such a project, which would have made the rival organisation more effective. After several disagreements with the Webbs on policy and organisational issues, he eventually broke with the Fabians over their failure to denounce the South African War. He formally resigned from the executive in 1900.

Meanwhile, in 1896, he married Margaret Ethel Gladstone, a young lady of good connections. Her father was an academic and a prominent Liberal in London politics, and her mother, long deceased, was the niece of Lord Kelvin. Margaret had a religious background, and had early involved herself in evangelicalism and social work in the East End. By the early 1890s she was looking for something more in her life. She had not chosen to sit around and wait for marriage, but there was still an aspect of her personality which was not fulfilled. She confided her feelings to her diary, and of her emotional prospects she enquired: 'I wonder whether I shall meet him in this world. I mean, my him, my sir, my knight. If love lasts on to another world for those whose souls are married here, can we believe that God leaves some souls always unmarried?'. MacDonald was to be the answer to her emotional needs.

She was already a committed socialist by the time she met MacDonald in 1895, and in the year of their marriage she joined the ILP. Thereafter they were to enjoy a political as well as a personal partnership, and their home was the meeting-place for gatherings of socialist leaders, radical intellectuals, trade unionists and other members of London's 'progressive' class. She knew him as Ramsay, the name his mother used; from 1896, the nomenclature was the one by which he was popularly known within his social circle.

In the closing years of the century he did much political writing, although his columns were anonymous. He also strengthened his position within the ILP, joining three other illegitimate Scotsmen, Bruce Glasier, Hardie and Snowden, to make up the 'big four'. All of them were journalists as well as would-be Westminster politicians. In 1899 he refused nomination for the chairmanship, but he gained prominence in the emerging Labour Movement through his opposition to the South African War, the cause of his resignation from the Fabian Society. Its members refused to issue a condemnation of government policy, for it was their practice not to make public statements on current affairs. He was vocal in his denunciations. He disapproved of imperialism, believing that 'further extensions of empire are only the grabbings of millionaires on the hunt'. The South African War was, in his view, an example of the corruption and trickery which accompanied imperialism, and he felt that it was unjust and unnecessary. His criticism did not centre only on the motivations of those involved in South African politics, but also on the peculiar horror of the fighting which saw the first use of concentration camps. War was an outrage against humanity, and although he was never an outright pacifist there was a markedly pacific strand within his approach to issues of international diplomacy.

By the end of the year, however, he was primarily involved on the domestic scene, in an enterprise which was to prove highly significant for the future of Labour as a political cause, as well as to his own prospects of political advancement – the formation of the Labour Representation Committee (LRC).

THE FORMATION OF THE LRC

Along with Hardie, MacDonald was much involved in the negotiations which led to the formation of the Labour Representation Committee. He helped to draft the resolution of the Parliamentary Committee of the Trade Union Congress to convene 'a special Congress . . . to devise ways and means for securing the return of an increased number of Labour members to the next Parliament'. In January 1900 that meeting was held, and 117 trade union delegates were joined by members of the Fabian Society, the ILP and the SDF; altogether, they represented just over half a million people. Marquand has divided those present into four broad categories: the Marxist contingent (mainly from the SDF), the Lib-Lab union leaders who might not have been too sorry to see the new experiment fail, the more advanced trade unionists who wanted to see the party succeed but were worried by the presence of so many convinced socialists, and finally the ILP – led still by Hardie – whose influence was on most matters decisive.

According to Hardie, the purpose of the meeting was to form 'a distinct Labour group in Parliament, who shall have their own whips, and agree upon their policy'. The Committee was the outcome, but at the time there was no reason to assume that this initiative would be significantly more successful than previous ones. The new body was not obviously a healthy one. It had no money, no agreed programme and only lukewarm support in the ranks of the wider labour movement.

Socialists and unions were to run and finance their candidates separately, and there was a need to ensure that their approach was coordinated. MacDonald had no difficulty in securing the secretaryship of the infant body, and it was his task to bring about such unity of purpose and activity. He was elected unanimously to what was initially an unpaid post, and in the early days he operated from a room in his Holborn flat. This was the unpromising beginning of his full-time political career, which was to see him establish Labour as a major force in British politics and become its first prime minister. The omens did not look good in 1900, and in many ways his job seemed a thankless task. Yet he shouldered his responsibilities with much skill and dedication until 1911, and in retrospect it can be seen that it was this office which provided him with a decisive political break.

The LRC received a surprising boost from a legal judgement in the House of Lords concerning the Taff Vale Railway Company. The state of the law regarding trade unions had already been shown to be unclear in several previous legal cases, but in this one the company had decided to sue the union for the loss of income and inconvenience it had incurred during a prolonged strike in South Wales. On appeal to the House of Lords, the Law Lords decided in favour of the company, and awarded it damages of £23 000 against the union for the losses endured. The decision was a damaging blow to trade unionists for it made the organisation of strikes futile. Any gains won by the union in a strike would be at the cost of severely weakening union finances, so that the strike weapon would in future prove to be ineffective and costly. After the verdict, trade unionists could see the point of increased parliamentary representation, and many joined the LRC in the months after the Taff Vale judgement. The Amalgamated Society of Engineers (the union involved in the dispute), textile workers and many other unskilled workers were brought within the fold.

By 1903, MacDonald was acting as secretary on behalf of 861 000 members, a majority of the organised trade union movement. One of his early and important tasks was to negotiate an agreement with Herbert Gladstone, the Liberal Chief Whip and son of the party's most distinguished prime minister. At its 1903 conference the LRC had, among other things, decided its candidates must 'strictly abstain from identifying themselves with or promoting the interests of any section of the Liberal or Conservative parties'. Its independence thus established, MacDonald nonetheless saw merit in concluding a secret deal with the Liberals in order that LRC candidates would not face Liberal opposition in the next election, which would have split the anti-Conservative vote and made the election of Unionists a greater probability. In 1903 the task seemed more urgent because of the possible imminence of a general election given the government's disunity over the tariff issue. Joseph Chamberlain was urging his fellow

Unionists to impose protective measures (a programme known as 'tariff reform') against goods imported from outside the Empire, whereas like the Liberals the LRC took up the cause of free trade, which was identified with a policy of cheap food. Although Unionist divisions worsened, there was no early election.

Both sides saw benefit in the electoral agreement. Gladstone was eager to come to terms with the infant party, hoping that the deal would limit the damage which it could inflict on the Liberals. MacDonald believed that it provided the basis to establish the LRC as an independent political force in its own right. He knew there would be opposition in the constituencies, so that the agreement needed to be kept secret to prevent irreconcilables in both parties from wrecking it. At the time relations on the ground between LRC and Liberal candidates were often rather poor, for in both parties many local organisations preferred to run candidates and fight to the finish.

Apart from MacDonald, Hardie was probably the only other national figure who was 'in the know' about the Lib-Lab pact. But the agreement held, and was made the more possible because a number of issues arose in 1904–5 on which the two parties shared broadly similar approaches. There was a common dislike of the 1902 Education Act (seen as damaging to the interests of the nonconformists), a profound dislike for Chinese slavery (the introduction of cheap Chinese labour into South Africa), and of course agreement on the overriding issues of tariffs, the principal controversy of the period. Joseph Chamberlain, the Colonial Secretary until 1903, firmly believed in the desirability of tariffs as the best way of reviving British prosperity following the years of the so-called 'Great Depression' at the end of the nineteenth century, and his proposals would have meant taxes on food from countries outside the Empire. Labour joined with the Liberals in opposition to what they saw as a 'stomach tax', and the Unionist Government was seriously divided over the policy, Chamberlain and others resigning to argue their case. The issue rallied the Liberals and was a bonus for both opposition parties who saw tariff reform as detrimental to the interests of working men.

Despite some common approaches, ILP militants were especially keen to see open contests occur in the next election, for most members were strongly opposed to the Liberals. It was pointed out to them that several people in the LRC did not belong to the ILP anyway, and that if

ILP candidates were to run against Liberals then there would be no financial support from the London headquarters. Such considerations helped to win the doubters over and, when the election came in 1906, the success of the pact was apparent. Of 50 LRC candidates (ten sponsored by the ILP), only 18 were opposed by Liberal candidates, and some of those were not opposed by official ones. In ten constituencies where there were two members, a Liberal and an LRC candidate found themselves fighting side by side, and this high level of cooperation proved most effective. The LRC gained 29 victories, 12 in Lancashire where joint action was particularly well-developed. In areas like Yorkshire and Wales, it was more limited, for the Liberal Party had a strong base and the LRC found it difficult to make much impact. In Scotland, where Liberals were more entrenched and where the National Liberal Federation had no influence, the agreement did not operate.

In those early years, MacDonald threw himself into his office as secretary with enormous energy and dedication, even before he gained any payment for the task. He spoke at meetings, organised activities and wrote party literature, and out of almost nothing he created a viable, if rudimentary, organisation. The resolution carried at the 1905 conference was a justified tribute to the quality of his performance. Moved by two trade unionists, it read:

> That this Congress hereby places on record its hearty appreciation of the valuable services rendered to our movement by J. R. MacDonald, Secretary of the LRC, and assures him that the success of our educational work in the country is in no small measure due to the tireless energy he has displayed not merely in the general organising work in the several districts, but also to the literature issued dealing with the various social problems.

Yet despite such generous praise, he had contemplated giving up early in 1903, believing that 'the preliminary work of launching this movement has now been completed . . . I have a great deal of work on hand, and for some years I have been hoping to do certain things which I see with much regret slipping further and further away . . . My inclination is to try and get some leisure time for myself'. He was persuaded to carry on, for as Glasier put it: 'We have no man [in the ILP], and there is none in the trade unions to take your place.' Perhaps it is significant that it was in the following year that he was given a small increase in funding to enable a salary to be paid to him personally (£150) and to others who assisted.

LIFE AS AN MP

MacDonald's personal prospects were enhanced with his election in 1906 as an MP in the two-member constituency of Leicester. He had already stood as a candidate there in the election of 1900 and was heavily defeated, but he had got elected to the London County Council as the member for Central Finsbury in 1901 as a representative of the 'Progressive and Labour interests in the area'. His membership of the ILP and his disagreements with Sidney Webb over the provision of technical education (he saw Webb as too pro-government) prevented his nomination as a governor of University College, London.

In the 1906 Parliament he was one of a group of seven ILP members, who also included Keir Hardie and Philip Snowden. After the election, he wrote in his secretarial capacity to members of the Executive Committee of the LRC (and to his fellow members) to tell them that a joint meeting was to be convened. It would discuss various organisational details, such as their seating in the House and the attitude of the LRC members to other Labour MPs. He also proposed to discuss with the members alone the issue of the chairmanship, arrangements for whipping and regular meetings of the groups. It was accepted by the LRC that the vacancy was a matter for MPs alone, for the chairman's primary responsibility was to serve as spokesman for his fellow MPs and to organise the work of the party in the House. In no sense was the post considered to be leader of the party as a whole, so the LRC did not concern itself with the issue. In the same year as the election, he was elected chairman of the ILP, a position he held until 1909. It was his work in that role which earned him the glowing tribute from Hardie that he was 'the biggest intellectual asset which the socialist movement had in this country today'.

The success in 1906 was sensational at the time and caused alarm in governing circles. The defeated Unionist Prime Minister, Arthur Balfour, saw the Liberal Prime Minister, Campbell-Bannerman, as a 'mere cork' on the socialist tide. Yet such language was unmerited, and interested observers such as the Fabian playwright, George Bernard

Shaw, felt that it was the other way round, the LRC being the cork on an overwhelming Liberal tide.

MacDonald's own reaction to the 1906 result was to write that: 'Everybody is asking: "What does it all mean? What does the Labour Party want? What will it do?"' He went on to predict that the party '[would] have a hand in the making of history'. This was not immediately obvious, and the party failed to impress in Parliament. Indeed, life soon proved difficult and demoralising for Labour members who were unable to establish an independent indentity. On many issues the 53 working men were in agreement with the Liberal government in the coming years, and it was difficult for them to show themselves to be distinct. They could hardly oppose measures which individual socialists had long espoused, and to abstain was an inglorious option which would not be understood outside the movement by working people in the country. MacDonald personally was ready to accept social reforms which were passed, as a useful step for the time being whilst his party pursued a socialist utopia for the future.

A further difficulty was that the phalanx of working-class MPs was a motley crew whose members disagreed on many key items. It was hard to impose effective leadership, and neither Hardie (chairman from 1906–8), nor Henderson (1908–10), nor Barnes (1910–11) was able to establish a strong ascendancy. It was common for members to split three ways in their voting habits. Indeed, in 1907 Hardie established the principle that in cases in which an MP's individual conscience troubled him, he was allowed to vote as he wished.

Pelling has noted that the Labour Party 'was largely deficient in parliamentary and administrative talent, and was incapable of producing satisfactory alternative policies of its own'. Labour MPs were all of working-class origin and, though some of them were quite able men, they lacked professional training and experience of running things. They had as yet no middle-class Fabians in the ranks, and in any case they distrusted the Fabian leaders because of their readiness to 'permeate' the older political parties with their ideas.

There was tension in the relationship between Hardie and MacDonald, who both in their distinctive ways made such immense contributions to the building of the Labour Party. Hardie ranked first in seniority and in the magnitude of his contribution to the building of the party. Hardie saw himself as the inspiration and guiding hand of the party which he had done so much to bring into being, and he detected signs that others such as MacDonald might allow it to stray from the course he wished to chart. MacDonald found himself operating in the shadow of a much venerated older man who was reluctant to let go the reins. He felt frustrated, for he wanted to impart more cohesion and organisational strength to the substantial new group of Labour MPs.

At times, MacDonald despaired of Hardie's performance, even though he cooperated loyally with him. He was exasperated by Hardie's non-attendance at meetings, and in early 1907 he noted that 'the elements of discord are gathering in a most menacing way'. It seems that MacDonald was contemplating the prospect of the chairmanship as far back as 1907, even if his socialist predilections made his election unlikely. In that year, he wrote to Glasier that:

> It would be a little awkward, at present, to put a 'mere' Socialist in the chair because it might hinder the prospect of consolidation . . . I am not in the least afraid of facing the leadership. But to take the job on for a period of two years, at the most, is a bit discouraging for a start. The chief question we shall have to settle is: 'Would it be better to give an old gang leader a chance after Hardie and get a Socialist in two years from now (if we could) or take just as much as a majority vote will give us at present?'.

ANXIETIES ON THE LEFT, 1906–11

There were many troubles and tribulations for the Labour Party in these years, but a key issue among them centred on the attitude of the Labour Party to the Liberal government. In 1907, Hardie had advised the Annual Conference that there was little point in 'running amok at the Treasury Bench', and MacDonald had taken the view that in the first years or so it was important to have a quiet parliamentary session in which MPs might adjust to life in the House and learn how to use parliamentary opportunities most effectively. It seemed wise to concentrate on putting down detailed amendments on what were specifically labour issues, on which they might hope to achieve some influence, and use their discretion on others as they arose. This form of response, that of a parliamentary pressure group prodding the Liberals in the right direction on issues of concern, was not one which was popular with many outside the House. The extra-parliamentary socialists were restive, and felt that the MPs' association with the Liberals was limiting the scope to establish a clear identity. This feeling was expressed by Victor Grayson who described himself as a 'clean socialist' and won a three-cornered by-election in a former Liberal seat, Colne Valley. His stirring oratory roused feeling that the working class was ready for revolution. Although the ILP had originally disowned him, his election confirmed that there were many in the movement who were uneasy about the direction of affairs. MacDonald had reservations about Grayson's qualities, particularly his reliability, but he tried to integrate him into the Labour Party for fear of a widening gulf developing between the differing elements in the party.

MacDonald's own performances were often impressive. They usually contained little reference to socialist ideology – too little for some of his followers – but he was effective in making interventions in debate and in putting down amendments. One initiative which earned him much praise was in relation to the Unemployed Workmen Bill. The Conservatives had legislated ineffectually in 1905, setting up local distress committees to help those out of work. Though deficient, the statute was at least a recognition that the state should help its citizens to find work. The measure was due to expire in 1907, and in July of that year MacDonald put forward a more radical proposal on behalf of the Labour Party. It was brief and ill-drafted, but its importance was that it stressed that the right to work was a basic one in any civilised society. Moreover, it was to be the duty of local authorities to find employment for those in need of a job and if they were unable to do so then they must make provision for the maintenance of families affected by the absence of an income.

Inevitably the attempt failed, but over the winter there was growing support for its principles. A Liberal MP took up the issue in a private member's bill. Glasier urged MacDonald to make a strong stand in its defence during the second reading ('Fight, fight, fight – do not give way on any point to the Government'), and MacDonald took up the challenge with relish. He felt deeply about the indignity of unemployment, and his speech in support of the Bill was one of his best in the House in these early years. He recalled his own experiences, wandering 'from workshop to workshop begging to be employed, and going home every day without anything found, feeling a horrible sense that one was abandoned by his neighbours'. He dismissed the view that unemployment was caused by fecklessness and lack of effort, and pointed out that in a capitalist economy it was inevitable, given the regular cycle of boom and recession. Because of this it was the duty of society to ensure that those made redundant should 'not be trodden down to destruction'.

This second attempt at legislation was also unsuccesful, but MacDonald, as the main exponent of the case for the unemployed, made a profound impression on many who heard him. A fellow Labour MP, Clynes, later remembered 'the unusual amount of interest in the House', and wrote of the fighting spirit with which the speech was delivered. Yet such parliamentary activity was unrewarding, in the sense that Labour – for all its good intentions – was in no position to achieve results. Parliamentary life was proving to be very frustrating.

MacDonald was often critical about trade union MPs, many of whom were ineffective speakers and poor at exploiting parliamentary opportunities, yet the ILP leadership of which he was a part was officially supporting the alliance of Labour members. Some ILP members were urging the adoption of more overtly socialist policies, and there was an increasing wish among some of them to adopt a radical strategy. In 1908, MacDonald expounded his own brand of socialism which was not easily distinguishable from the position of some of the more radical New Liberals. It was to be 'a guiding idea for legislation, for administration, for all constructive work of a social character'. The emphasis in his *Socialism and Government* (1909) was on what Austin Morgan calls 'parliamentary evolutionism', and the writer went on to observe that by this approach 'the goal of a Socialist society was thereby theoretically liquidated'. What emerged clearly in the two-volume book was a distaste for any form of exhibitionism which 'would degrade the House of Commons', the sort of behaviour which had led to the suspension of Grayson in 1908. The left-winger had made a protest over unemployment in a debate on the Licensing Bill, and when ruled 'out of order' refused to yield. MacDonald derided the attempt to emulate 'the dramatic force of Henry Irvine' (a famous contemporary actor).

MacDonald and Hardie both quickly realised that the ILP could be a thorn in the flesh, and in 1909 they, Snowden and Glasier all resigned from its Council in a test of strength. They were troubled by the increasing irresponsibility of ILP members who seemed content to go their own way whatever the views of the leading figures in the party. When the 'big four' announced their resignations there was a desperate plea on the part of ILP MPs to persuade them to stay in office, but no amount of persuasion – even a rendition of 'Will ye no' come back again?' – could win Hardie and the others round.

The ILP was clearly a gathering force, and in the 1910 pamphlet *Let Us Reform the Labour Party* (known as the Green Manifesto because of the colour of its cover) the writers boldly proclaimed that 'Labour must stand for Socialism and its own hand against BOTH the capitalist parties IMPARTIALLY'. Such men did not have control of ILP, but they were a powerful force within it. A number of them seceded from the ILP, and formed a rival British Socialist Party in 1911.

A new challenge on the left came from the syndicalists. Syndicalism was a militant movement which had grown up inside the unions. Its adherents despaired of making gains via the parliamentary battle. Prominent among them was Tom Mann, he of 1889 Dock Strike fame. Like others, he wished to seize control of the economy via industrial action and it was the unions who could bring this about. Syndicalism derived from two philosophical roots. On the one hand, there was Daniel de Leon, an American Marxist who preached the language of class warfare. A French inspiration was provided by the writings of Georges Sorel who advocated the use of the general strike as a means of undermining capitalism. If the influence of the creed upon the Labour Movement was never vast in terms of membership, it had an important input. It made an impression on a young generation of trade union leaders, especially the miners who were increasingly impatient with the moderate Labour leadership.

Syndicalism and other left-wing views were expressed via the *Daily Herald*, a new labour daily newspaper that came into being. George Lansbury, nominally a member of the ILP, was a key figure in its creation and early development, and throughout the pre-war period a very fine cartoonist, Will Dyson, used his chosen form to vent his anger and ferocity in savage drawings. Dyson was an ideologue, and as an uncompromising socialist he lambasted the reformist traditions of the Labour Party and ridiculed the British ruling classes. An official Labour newspaper, the *Daily Citizen*, was far more orthodox in its outlook. Backed by the TUC, it began publication in 1912. Its funds were less imperilled, but it was less inspirational. (When war broke out in 1914, it immediately ceased publication whereas the *Herald* survived and continued to grow in strength when the war was over.)

THE CHAIRMANSHIP, 1911–14

In the years after 1906, MacDonald recognised that the trade union MPs exhibited minimal interest in socialist theory, and that for the while the chances of his election to the chairmanship were small. But he had little respect for those who were in charge of Labour's parliamentary fortunes. Along with Glasier, he was relieved when Hardie stood down in 1908, but both of them felt that Arthur Henderson, his successor (1908–10) was so eager to identify the party with the Liberal government that he was unable to act as a driving force. In their eyes, he appeared on Liberal platforms too often, and they disliked his strong association with the union members of the party. Hardie had been unacceptable to many unionists, and Henderson was inappropriate for many in the ILP. As for his successor, George Barnes, they deemed him to be a 'disastrous failure'. Barnes had been willing to back MacDonald in 1910, but in the middle of the discussions between those involved MacDonald suffered the first of his shattering bereavements (see pages 32–3). Quite how Barnes emerged as the first choice is uncertain, but what is clear is that MacDonald soon found his leadership inadequate and lacking in any sense of direction.

Barnes fell ill and did not stand in 1911. MacDonald was chosen as his replacement, at the age of 44. He had claimed the previous year that he did not want the chairmanship. Among his reservations was the thought that he might have been more effective as secretary than as chairman, the more so if the chairman's period was to end within two years. Moreover, he had another concern, the lack of unity and the irresponsibility in the party which he felt had developed under Keir Hardie's influence. In late 1910, he had written to Glasier to tell him that he saw nothing in it 'but vexation of spirit and barreness of effort'. Yet if he had misgivings, in the same letter he seemed to recognise the inevitable and he went on to explain his position: 'I shall not lead as a great many people want, because I shall say what I mean, whereas so many of our folks want declamation, stage dressing, paint and daggers in the belt.'

According to Snowden's autobiography, MacDonald had at about the same time written to him to protest that he on no account wanted the position: 'In view of the disloyal action of certain of our colleagues, I see no prospect of the Chairman being of the least use.' Such protestations are less than fully convincing, for Snowden records that within a few days he was receiving a further enquiry from MacDonald as to 'how the land lay'. MacDonald recognised that if he made overt enquiries then he could be accused of self-interest and undue ambition, but he hoped that Snowden could take discreet soundings. The latter was unenthusiastic, and informed the would-be chairman that he tended to keep clear of all party intrigues.

For Lord Elton, there was remarkably little personal ambition in MacDonald's attitude to the leadership: 'Seldom can a more reluctant leader have been elected.' Certainly, there were reasons as to why anyone might be a reluctant hero, not least the unrewarding task of leading such a divided group as the PLP. Yet party leaders often claim that they never sought office and that they only allowed their name to go forward for the good of the party, in the absence of a convincing alternative. Snowden's evidence suggests that MacDonald was no less unwilling than many others have been. As it was, he allowed himself to be persuaded, flattered no doubt by a group of ILP colleagues who told him that he had done more to influence the thinking and organisation of the Labour–Socialist alliance than any one else.

MacDonald took over at the start of the new parliamentary session in January 1911, following the general election of December 1910. A deal was done by which MacDonald was to relinquish the secretaryship which Henderson had long wanted, and MacDonald would assume the treasurership and thereby remain on the party Executive. In 1912, both moves were confirmed, and MacDonald was to continue to hold on to his treasurer's position until 1930. Whatever the intensity of his ambition, he was aware of the task ahead, and on the eve of taking over he was writing 'I see nothing but storms and heartaches ahead'.

THE PARLIAMENTARY SITUATION, 1911–14

As in the first election at the beginning of 1910, in December the Liberal government had failed to win a parliamentary majority and needed Labour and Irish support. Labour was in a position to exact concessions, and one of its priorities was to see legislation to reverse the Osborne Judgement of 1909. This was a legal decision of the House of Lords which struck a great blow to the Labour Party. Osborne, a Liberal trade unionist, had brought a court case challenging the right of his union, the Railway Servants, to give money to political parties – knowing that the party which benefited was one he personally opposed, Labour. He won, and the effect was to prevent unions from making such political contributions. The verdict in the Upper House had a great effect on the finances of the Labour Party, which depended almost entirely on such income. Once the Liberal government needed Labour support (following its weakened position in 1910), Labour could press for a concession on this matter which was of great importance to it. A Trade Union Act of 1913 allowed unions to raise funds for political purposes, as long as they had a separate political fund from their general/industrial one. Trade unionists could contract out of paying the political levy, but the general assumption was that the members of affiliated unions would pay it whether or not they wished to do so, once the onus was on them to request that no such payment was made.

MacDonald had been bitterly critical of the failure of the Asquith government to act to reverse the Osborne decision back in 1909–10. He saw inaction as 'tantamount to a declaration of war . . . [The Government] is to stand supinely by whilst trade unionism is being imprisoned within such narrow bounds that it cannot meet with any success the attacks that are now being made upon it'. For him, the issue had been so important that he had urged his Labour colleagues to adopt a more determined and hostile position to ministers unless they showed a greater willingness to legislate. The passage of the Act in 1913 was therefore an important prize which the party had been able to demand.

MacDonald also succeeded in pressing the case for payment of MPs which eventually came about in 1911, but Labour won little else. The Liberals had their own legislative programme and in return for the move on Members' salaries MacDonald offered to support the National

Insurance Bill which was designed to set up a state scheme of compulsory insurance for workers against sickness and unemployment. He personally believed that the contributory principle which underlay it was appropriate, remarking during the passage of the Bill that he favoured insurance and not a 'free gift'. Such views did not meet with the approval of Snowden, Lansbury and several other prominent Labour spokesmen. They wanted a more costly but more comprehensive National Health Service, undertaking preventive work for the benefit of the whole community. Whilst most of the members of the PLP agreed with MacDonald's position and supported the Liberals in the voting lobbies, some refused to go along with it.

In spite of the insurance disagreement, MacDonald had some success in his plea for increased discipline within the party in the House of Commons. Very soon after taking over as chairman he circulated a letter to his colleagues in which he set out his approach to matters of party organisation in the House. Three issues bothered him, the 'foolish criticism passed upon us by our members in the country', 'the slackness of individual members in the House of Commons' and 'the lack of party cohesion and of a general enthusiastic backing of each individual Member, either when he is attacked or is attacking, in the House of Commons'.

In the communication, he noted the way in which members in other parties encouraged and supported their spokesmen, and pointedly observed that: 'A demonstration of the virile unity of a party is just as important as the speeches of its members.' Amongst other things, he called for:

- Greater loyalty in the House.
- An increased work-rate from Labour MPs.
- A greater willingness to participate in debates: 'Over-speaking is a vice, but so is under-speaking . . . The habit of sitting on benches is easily lost and members should strenuously strive against losing it, as if that happens Party efficiency becomes very poor indeed'.
- Better attendance at weekly party meetings.
- More regular speaking on platforms outside the House, giving interviews etc.

By such exhortations and the force of his own example, MacDonald had some success in bringing about a greater sense of solidarity and cohesion in the Parliamentary Party. His own performances were powerful in their impact, for at 46 he was at the height of his powers having overcome his initial qualms about speech-making in the chamber. He was the star performer on the Labour side and only Snowden could approach him in his effectiveness as a parliamentarian. As chairman of a party whose support the government needed, he was not without influence, and he was acquiring a reputation as a significant player in British political life.

But in the pre-war years it was not apparent that the Liberal government and eventually the Liberal Party was doomed, and there was no obvious prospect of greater political advance for MacDonald or his party. He became frustrated and disillusioned with his office, for he felt that there was little satisfaction to be gained from 'shepherding its [Labour's] ranks so that they did not become a disorganised mob'. If he was depressed (and it was always a tendency within his make-up), on this occasion he had good reason to be so. In personal terms the years 1910–11 had been ones of immense sadness and loneliness.

PUBLIC INVOLVEMENT AND FAMILY BEREAVEMENT
—

MacDonald was on good terms with a number of Liberal MPs and some ministers as well. His parliamentary duties and his political socialising had left him little time for home and family life, and after 1906 he had seen much less of his wife and children. After his assumption of the chairmanship, the demands on his time were to grow even more pressing, and for a while in 1911–12 there was even a suggestion that he might join a coalition government. MacDonald was unwilling to commit himself to supporting the Liberals 'through thick and thin', but he did not rule out the prospect in the future.

His wife too had been busily involved in public life, showing especial interest in the rights of working women. She also supported 'votes for women', as did MacDonald, though neither of them had much sympathy for the activities of the militant suffragettes. Above all, Margaret MacDonald was concerned to increase opportunities to involve women in the Labour Movement, even though she recognised much value in the contribution made by women at home and in the workplace.

In 1910–11, tragedy hit Ramsay MacDonald. His youngest son died of diphtheria in 1910, quickly followed to the grave by MacDonald's mother in Lossiemouth. Then in the middle of 1911 his wife died of heart failure, following a severe case of blood poisoning. This was a blow from which MacDonald never fully recovered, and his sense of loss was always with him. Some of his feelings were penned in a book which appeared in 1912, but the public expression of grief did nothing to rid him of his feelings of loneliness and sadness.

THE PRE-WAR THREAT TO PARLIAMENTARY GOVERNMENT

The years immediately before 1914 were difficult for the Liberal government, for it was confronted by militant trade unionists intent upon using industrial action, by peers in the House of Lords over the passage of the Parliament Bill, by Ulster Protestants in the markedly deteriorating situation in Ireland and by revolting women. Liberal England found it difficult to cope with such a major series of problems, and in the years before the war there was an atmosphere of political crisis for much of the time. Reason and moderation seemed to be under attack, as the disaffected women, trade unionists and Ulstermen resorted to extra-parliamentary forms of pressure in a bid to force the hand of ministers.

In such circumstances, MacDonald stuck to his firm commitment to parliamentary methods. Lacking the background of trade unionists from the industrial working class, he was out of sympathy with displays of industrial strife, and he used his influence with union leaders to try and achieve industrial harmony via conciliation. He might share some of their goals and was willing to support a minimum wage for groups such as the miners, but in 1912 he felt able to accuse the militant leaders of the London dockers of 'plunging the whole country into a state of unsettlement'.

He disapproved of syndicalism, for he was more preoccupied with the national interest than were those syndicalist leaders who preached class warfare. In *Syndicalism: A Critical Examination* (1912) he defined the idea as 'British trade unionism applied to revolutionary purposes', and he made plain his preference for gradualist methods: 'Society is in a process of change, and the workers who are toiling for greater justice are only retarding progress by following the wrong-doing of which they are victims, rather than strengthening the social tendencies which make for their emancipation'. The book was well-received, not least by many members in the other parties who saw the intervention as a helpful condemnation of extremist action.

He understood the reasons for social tension, and in 1913 wrote another volume on contemporary discontents, *The Social Unrest: Its Cause and Solution*. Here he put the prevailing strife in a historical context, and having concluded that the threat from syndicalism had largely passed away he concentrated on elaborating his own preferred methods. He saw merit in guild socialism, by which workers' control of industry could be promoted. This variety placed less emphasis on the role of the state than did Fabianism, though more than did the majority of syndicalists. The state would have remained ultimately supreme, but much power would have been delegated to industrial guilds. Guild members would have been provided with a range of welfare benefits, and each guild would have paid a single tax or rent to the government. Whatever his willingness to embrace such new forms of industrial organisation, he was unwilling to countenance militancy as a way of promoting socialist goals.

THE THREAT OF WAR
——

In addition to the other difficulties of the Liberal government before 1914, the threat of war loomed on the horizon. Most Labour MPs, like many Liberals, worried about spending on armaments, and saw such expenditure as a futile diversion of funds better spent on social improvement. On foreign policy generally, they did not show particular interest, and the trade union element in the party did not generally concern itself with the question.

Some socialists were more involved in international issues for the Labour Party was affiliated to the Socialist International, which, with its large German contingent, was pledged to agitate against war. Idealists felt that given a conflict of national interests and international class solidarity, then the latter would win. They opposed any increase in armaments, although Labour MPs who represented dockyard constituencies sometimes took a different line because of the issue of unemployment. In general Labour MPs were ill-informed on matters of international diplomacy and several had little knowledge or understanding of Britain's international commitments. The Liberal government offered little information about the military and naval agreements concluded with France, so that Labour spokesmen offered few informed and worthwhile observations.

MacDonald was one of the better-informed among them. He had been interested in overseas policy as far back as the 1890s, and his internationalism was well established as a result of his attendance at a number of gatherings of European socialist leaders. Beyond such personal contacts, he enjoyed travel abroad, was sympathetic to foreigners and was willing to listen when Europeans criticised British policy. Such leanings were not the basis of any coherently thought-out ideas, but they made him suspicious of the force of nationalism and contemptuous of war as a means of resolving international disputes. Inasmuch as there were any signs of belligerence in British policy, he was likely to be against it, and as war loomed nearer he increasingly disapproved of the Liberal government's diplomacy. In particular, he disliked ministers' sympathy towards the Tsarist regime in Russia, and their attitude to German affairs. He believed that they should have been more supportive of those opposition elements in Germany who were opposed to militarism, whereas the Foreign Office – in his view – made little attempt to distinguish between the Kaiser's government and the German people.

MacDonald was nearly 48 when war broke out, so that he had already spent many years in active political work. Indeed, more of his career in politics was behind him than ahead of him, although it is a period which has often been neglected by those who prefer to dwell on his later actions as Prime Minister. In this lengthy section of his life certain aspects of his contribution stand out. He was – along with Hardie – largely the architect of the 'Labour Alliance' of socialists and trade unionists which came together in the LRC. He then proved himself to be Labour's main organiser and strategist, the man who had charted the course of the new party from 1900 onwards. It was he who was a key element in that association between a more radical Liberal government and the growing Labour parliamentary pressure group which Kenneth Morgan has described as the 'Progressive Alliance'. The agreement of 1903 enabled the party to establish a strong foothold in Parliament, and thereafter MacDonald worked with reform-minded Liberals to bring about social improvement, whilst shunning the 'extremism' of more militant socialists.

Secondly, by his writings and speeches, he had emerged as Labour's leading theorist, and if some of his literary output lacks originality it remains as a useful statement of early twentieth century evolutionary socialism. Labour already owed him a debt of gratitude in 1914, in itself worthy of credit even if later the value of some of his life's work was to be undermined.

timeline	1866	born in Lossiemouth
	1886	moves to London
	1892	socialist views set out in *The New Charter*
	1894	fails to be adopted as Lib-Lab candidate; joins ILP; elected to Fabian Executive
	1895	ILP candidate at Southampton
	1900	resigns from Fabian Executive over South African War; formation of Labour Representation Committee, MacDonald secretary
	1903	negotiates Lib-Lab electoral agreement with Herbert Gladstone
	1906	strong Labour presence in new House after Liberal landslide, MacDonald elected; LRC becomes Labour Party; chairmanship of ILP
	1907–08	fights for Unemployed Workmen Bill
	1911	chairman of Labour Party
	1912	treasurer of Labour Party.

Points to consider

1) What circumstances led to the rise of a specifically Labour Party at the turn of the twentieth century?
2) Why did MacDonald develop an interest in socialism? What were his main early socialist attitudes and beliefs?
3) What was MacDonald's attitude to the Liberal Party at the end of the nineteenth century and in the years before 1914?
4) In what ways was he effective as
    (a) an MP?
    (b) Party chairman, 1911–14?

3

FROM THE WAR TO THE PARTY LEADERSHIP

The outbreak of hostilities posed enormous problems for the Labour Party. Its key spokesmen had come out against war in the preceding months, and when it was declared on 4 August, the PLP was seemingly committed in its opposition to any British intervention. MacDonald spoke for many in the party and in a manner pleasing to members. He personally felt that the United Kingdom was in no danger from German aggression. In his view war would not have come about if there had not been a build-up of alliances on either side, and an obsession with the balance of power in Europe. Yet he was faced with the situation as it was, and recognised that fighting had become almost inevitable. When responding in the House of Commons to the Foreign Secretary's appeal for British support for the French, he replied:

> Whatever may happen, whatever may be said about us, we will take the action . . . of saying that this country ought to have remained neutral, because in the deepest parts of our hearts we believed that that was consistent with the honour of our country, and the traditions of the party that are now in office.

A day later, Belgium was invaded and this event transformed popular perceptions in the country. There was almost universal backing for war and those who were hitherto opponents came to see the necessity of making a firm stand against German plans. By 5 August, opinion in Labour's National Executive was no longer unanimous. A compromise resolution criticising the fact that Britain was committed to support for France 'without the knowledge of our people' was passed by eight votes to four, but did not directly oppose the war. Rather, it wanted the Labour Movement to 'secure peace at the earliest possible moment on such conditions as will provide the best opportunities for the re-establishment of amicable feelings between the workers of Europe'. The statement concealed deep divisions which were only papered over, for whilst most Labour MPs were disposed to support the war as a fact of life, the ILP leaders were clearly opposed. Such divisions were not unique to British socialists. In France and Belgium, socialist comrades were calling for resistance to the German invaders, and on the other side German Social Democrats voted for measures to support the German military.

MacDonald's position was untenable, and when it was known that on 6 August the Prime Minister was to move a resolution calling for support for war credits the party called a meeting for the night before. Labour decided not to oppose, and MacDonald tendered his resignation as chairman, though he remained on the NEC in his office as treasurer. Henderson took over, and offered broad Labour support for the duration of the war. A truce was called, suspending the party battle, and help was promised in the recruitment campaign. MacDonald did not feel that he could back the recruitment drive, and in late August he was to refuse to appear on a platform to call for more volunteers.

For MacDonald, resignation was a welcome release from the frustrations of leadership, and he recorded in his diary that he '[felt] that a great break [had] come'. He was less prepared for the venom which would be unleashed against him, and very quickly there were signs that he would suffer for his anti-war stance. He was attacked in the press for his criticism of the Foreign Secretary's conduct of affairs, and the criticism was made that by his observations he was undermining the national effort and encouraging the enemy. He became an increasingly solitary figure, so that suddenly the man close to government circles and consulted over key policies was cast aside as an outsider and rebel.

MacDonald did not oppose all war on principle, but felt that this one was unnecessary. He was never an outright pacifist, though he found war an abomination since both the fighting itself and the propaganda involved in the prosecution of war were a denial of the civilised values to which he was deeply attached. The outbreak of war shattered his hopes for peaceful and orderly progress towards the better society of which he dreamed. He felt that British policy had been wrong in several respects, and disapproved of the policies of imperialism, militarism and secret diplomacy pursued by the Liberal government over several years.

Resignation was a brave act, and he and his family suffered from it. He stood by as one prominent Labour spokesman after another joined the wartime administrations, and he became the victim of hostility from most sectors of political opinion. There was an exception to the general condemnation, however, for although his attitude damaged his standing in the country at large it did him no harm with members of the ILP. Five of its seven MPs opposed the war from a pacifist standpoint. It issued a *Manifesto on International Socialism*, in which it offered fraternal greetings to German socialists 'across the roar of guns'.

MacDonald, Hardie (who died in 1915) and other ILP leaders were a small and isolated group, supported only by a few Liberals. In September, he and four of them, including Charles Trevelyan and Arthur Ponsonby, formed the Union of Democratic Control (UDC) to campaign against the war and demand more democratic control of foreign policy, a negotiated peace, no annexations, parliamentary approval of the treaties and international machinery to facilitate peace and disarmament. Members realised that there was little or no hope that they could help to bring the war to an end, but they were concerned to ensure that when this happened there should be a basis in the post-war era of a just and lasting peace. As such, the organisation was a very suitable vehicle for a man such as MacDonald, and he much approved of the idea of people of broadly similar progressive views across the parties coming together in a joint crusade. Many middle class socialists within the Labour Party also believed that it was an ideal haven for those who wished to be involved in the bid to end the war, and a number of local Labour Party branches affiliated to it.

The expectation of many members of the Labour Movement was that war would not last, and it was hoped that party unity might survive in spite of serious differences of outlook. Henderson and his associates in the official party leadership had no wish to expel the pacifist element, for hopefully peacetime politics would soon return. Moreover, on both sides there was agreement about the alleged deficiencies of Sir Edward Grey's pre-war diplomacy. Henderson actually joined the UDC, though his membership was largely nominal. Several ILP leaders, including Snowden, remained aloof and opposed the war from a socialist rather than a broader popular perspective.

THE WARTIME COALITIONS

Such early cooperation began to disintegrate as the war dragged on. In May, Henderson was asked to join the Asquith Coalition government, and despite the reservations of many in the PLP the National Executive backed him. He entered the Cabinet as President of the Board of Education, and two other party figures took junior government office. In Austin Morgan's words, Henderson thereby 'became a prisoner of the war lords'. As such, he was forced to agree to several policies which were unpopular within the Labour Movement – such as the admission of unskilled workers into factory jobs previously reserved for trained craftsmen, and conscription. Henderson's presence did not prevent members of the industrial wing of the Labour Movement from taking unofficial industrial action, and on Clydeside feelings ran high. The 1916 Labour Conference came out against conscription.

The substitution of Lloyd George for Asquith in December 1916 made cooperation between Labour and the government easier, for when the new Prime Minister offered Henderson a place in the five-man War Cabinet, two ministerial seats and a number of junior offices, as well as pledges to take over the mines and shipping, this was too much to resist. By 1917 the cleavage in the party was widening, with some members actively supporting prosecution of the war effort, while the ILP was deeply opposed. Young ILP followers often resisted military service, and were taken into detention.

For MacDonald, the war years were a very difficult time, and the more the party officially backed the war effort the more isolated he became. Various ideas were mooted, and at the end of 1914 a Liberal MP had advised him to deploy his considerable organisational skills in the service of the Red Cross ambulance volunteer corps. He did actually go to Belgium to oversee the work of the agency and see the war at first hand. However, he had been arrested and deported. Shortly afterwards, he was able to see what was happening on the front, in a brief visit. But such involvement was far short of finding a role, and he spent much of the time in his public life writing and proclaiming his thoughts about war, acting as a political propagandist for the ILP. Within the House of Commons he said very little.

His anti-war stand won him much opprobrium among 'respectable' and popular opinion. As the war casualties mounted, those who took his position found themselves increasingly alone, and attacks on him ranged from the petty to the much more serious. Even in Lossiemouth, he was sent postcards by old acquaintances addressed to Herr Ramsay MacDonald; he was stoned when speaking at an ILP gathering; and he believed that the police were encouraging the disruption of his meetings to deny him a platform for his views. His personal fortunes reached a new low late in 1915, however, when the patriotic magazine, *John Bull*, ran the story that he was illegitimate, 'the son of a Scottish serving girl'. This was the culmination of a sustained campaign by the proprietor, Horatio Bottomley. Already it had denounced him as a 'pro-German' who 'whitewashed criminals in uniform', and as 'High Priest of Damnable Treason', a 'Traitor, Coward, Cur . . . [who should be] taken to the Tower and shot at dawn'. This MacDonald could bear with some fortitude, but then the criticism became even more malevolent. It went much further than before, for on 4 September 1915 an article appeared headed 'James Ramsay MacDonald. Leicester MP's name and origin – can he sit in Parliament?'. A birth certificate was portrayed, and from it MacDonald was able to see that he had been christened with the surname Ramsay. He thus learnt for the first time of his true origins; he had assumed that his father had left home after his birth, and now became aware that he had been born out of wedlock. His mother had already died and was spared the humiliation of the public revelation, but he felt 'the most terrible mental pain'. This was, of course, a time when the stigma of illegitimacy was much greater than it has been for many years, and the sort of people to whom Labour appealed – particularly those in the respectable working classes – would in many cases have been shocked by the revelation.

In some respects the vicious and scurrilous campaign backfired, for MacDonald received many letters of sympathy from within and outside the Labour Movement. Even the secretary of the National Union of Police and Prison Officers – not a natural ally of a radical anti-war politician – was moved to tender his 'sincere sympathy with you at the cowardly and outrageous personal attack of Mr Bottomley'. Such responses offered some consolation, but MacDonald's deep personal grief was intensified nearly a year later when some of the citizens in Lossiemouth organised a vote to get him expelled from the local golf club, lest he continue to 'endanger its character and interests'.

As the war continued, MacDonald began to despair of the future of the party, and found it hard to accept policies which the government (with official Labour approval) had introduced, particularly universal military service. In January 1917, union representatives at the Labour Conference attempted to restrict the influence of the socialist societies on the National Executive (by making the Executive electable by the whole Conference). Previously the unions and socialist groups each elected separate representatives. The passage of the motion by a narrow majority effectively meant the unions' domination of the Executive, for their voice was dominant at the Conference because of their block vote. MacDonald explained his approach in *Forward*, in a remark that illustrated the frustrations he felt then and was to feel later on with the behaviour and attitude of some within the party. He was:

> not going to sneak about and bargain for trade union votes for ILP candidates for the Executive . . . If a split were to come owing to the oppressive use of the block vote of some of the larger unions, I would do what I could to form a new Labour combination for political purposes.

Meanwhile, in January 1917 he wrote a slim volume setting out his opposition to war, *National Defence: A Study in Militarism.* In it, he articulated his thoughts about pacifism and the conduct of war. He again rejected an outright pacifist position, but still believed that in 1914 Britain's participation in the war had been wrong. Yet he was a realist and took the view that as the war was a fact of life 'we must go through with it'. He did not espouse a policy of defeatism, nor did he wish to see any form of revolution to end the armed struggle. He concentrated more on outlining his thinking about the need for a democratic foreign policy, which would be conducted in the open and not by secret negotiations and agreements. Above all, he argued for a return to the internationalist values of socialism which would help to secure this more democratic handling of diplomatic issues:

> The working classes must build up a Labour international diplomacy . . . which will be enforced and guaranteed by peoples in every European Parliament working in union with each other, insisting upon knowing what their Foreign Offices are doing and pursuing a common policy decided upon by themselves at joint conferences held frequently.

As it happened, events in the war took a very different turn. In March, the first Russian Revolution brought about the fall of the Tsar, a development widely welcomed by MacDonald and others in the Labour Movement. He felt that 'a sort of spring-tide had broken out all over the world'. The British government wanted to see Russia continue fighting and Henderson was despatched to Russia to ascertain feelings. He returned to urge cooperation with the Russians in the search for a negotiated peace, seeing this as the best means of persuading them to keep on fighting. He also wished to see British delegates attend an International Socialist Congress in Stockholm, at which German socialists would be present. His War Cabinet colleagues, however, disliked this initiative, and on being informed of their hostility and formally rebuked by Lloyd George, Henderson resigned in a state of considerable indignation. He had been kept waiting outside the door for over an hour whilst the issue was discussed (hence the title the 'doormat' incident). Although a Labour replacement – Barnes – was included in the War Cabinet, and the government retained the support of the Labour Party for the war effort, this was a decisive moment. Henderson, still Labour Party secretary, concentrated on party matters, and especially on the necessary work of reorganising the party machinery in preparation for the future general election.

Labour was still officially pro-war, but Henderson's resignation and other events, such as the successful Bolshevik Revolution of November 1917, brought about a change in the party's attitude to the war. The Bolsheviks were committed to ending Russian involvement in the hostilities, and with their withdrawal there was some reassessment of Labour thinking. The party was still part of the ruling Coalition, but the more radical unions (the miners and railway workers) began to campaign for a more independent Labour approach. The TUC was keen on a new initiative in foreign policy, and supported a document drawn up by Henderson with backing from Sidney Webb and MacDonald. This *Memorandum on War Aims* demanded new international arbitration machinery, the establishment of a League of Nations and other initiatives which would pave the way for future peace. If the new more distinctive approach cost Labour the backing of some pro-war union leaders, it won the approval of the Movement as a whole. The Lloyd George statement on war aims and the publication of

President Woodrow Wilson's Fourteen Points (January 1918) for a just and lasting peace reflected the influence of Labour thinking.

Henderson and Sidney Webb drew up a new constitution which would weld socialists and the union element more firmly together. As it adopted Clause Four it won the sympathy of socialists in the party, although there was little else about it which enthused them. MacDonald was unconvinced about the key importance attached to the union element within the party, and in a tract published by the ILP (1917) he had criticised union domination, seeing them as 'a terrible incubus on the Labour Party'. His disapproval was intensified by the way in which trade union associates had allowed themselves to be 'bought off' by the Coalition government.

In June 1918, a policy statement *Labour and the New Social Order* was approved by the Labour Conference. It called for policies based on four fundamental principles:

- **The concept of the national minimum** – a comprehensive policy of full employment, a minimum wage and a basic standard of working conditions with a maximum working week of 48 hours.
- **Democratic control of industry** – including the nationalisation of key industries.
- **A revolution in national finances** – involving heavy taxation of the rich to pay war costs and finance social expenditure.
- **The surplus for the common good** – the balance of the nation's wealth to be switched for use to increase educational and cultural opportunities for all.

The ceasefire was agreed in early October, although it was not until 11 November that the armistice was signed. Labour had already been busily selecting candidates in the preceding months, and armed with its new constitution and policy document it was in good shape for the forthcoming election whenever it should come.

THE 1918 ELECTION

When the war was over, the party had to decide on its attitude to its continuance in the Coalition. Those in the government (especially Barnes in the War Cabinet) were tempted by Lloyd George's suggestion that they remain in their place to play their part in making the peace. Clynes also felt that Labour representatives should stay in office until treaties were signed. Many Labour MPs were against this idea, and a special conference on 14 November 1918 called on participants to resign. Clynes did, Barnes and others refused and accordingly lost their party membership.

In December 1918 a general election was held. The odds were against a party which had not played a full part in the war effort, and out of a field of 361 Labour candidates only 57 were successful. As a result of the election, several able spokesmen disappeared, especially those who had opposed the war. MacDonald polled 6347 votes in West Leicester, as against 20510 for his Coalition opponent. The result was the more galling as the victor was a one-time member of the SDF but, like several others in that organisation, had abandoned his anti-militarist approach. Henderson, whose position had been more ambivalent, was also defeated so that of the more prominent spokesmen only Clynes survived.

MacDonald was very despondent about his defeat in West Leicester, 'sorry that [his] Parliamentary work [was] broken'. He had paid a heavy price for his attitude to the war. The hostility he endured took a heavy personal toll, as is apparent from his diary note in July 1918:

> Four years indignity, lying, blackguardism, have eaten like acid into me. Were I assassinated before it is all over would give no one who has followed the attacks cause for wonder.

1918–22

On his parliamentary defeat in 1918, MacDonald's work for the ILP became his main occupation. He continued to build up goodwill among fellow socialists, and his personal effectiveness in this role contrasted markedly with the ineffectiveness of Labour MPs in the House, a small much-outnumbered band. Many of these members were trade unionists whose talents did not include any capacity to provide credible and informed opposition. Moreover, mostly they were identified with the war. Their chairman, William Adamson, proved an unsatisfactory choice, and he had only emerged because a compromise was needed between Joseph Clynes and J. H. Thomas, who both had their respective proponents. As the representative of the miners, the largest section of the parliamentary party, Adamson gained wide acquiescence if not enthusiastic support.

MacDonald believed that 'the Labour team is altogether inadequately equipped for the part it ought to play'. What Adamson and his colleagues lacked and what MacDonald possessed in abundance were the essential parliamentary skills of making effective speeches and timely interventions, and organising tactical manoeuvres. In his autobiography, Snowden relates that at one point it was considered MacDonald might accept the position of general adviser to the parliamentary contingent. However, the suggestion was eventually turned down after a heated discussion, for the majority resented the prospect of being told how to conduct their own business. MacDonald was irritated by the rejection, and observed that 'it might be better to make a new combination and "smash" the present Labour Party'.

Busily engaged lecturing and writing as a way of earning his living, the immediate post-war years were a difficult time for MacDonald. He missed his wife very much and could not accept the idea of remarriage, but found little consolation in the company of men, particularly those in the Labour Movement. Other than his immediate family, whom he adored, he was a rather lonely figure. The MacDonalds were not made particularly welcome in Hampstead, where they had moved in 1916; probably the anti-war stance and ILP connections accounted for his isolation.

At this time he continued to be interested in international affairs. He was for a while broadly sympathetic to the new Soviet regime in Russia, and admired Lenin's capacity as an organiser and administrator. But he disliked the idea of revolution as a vehicle for social and political progress, noting among other considerations that revolutions inevitably turn into tyrannies. He preferred to work for a parliamentary majority, for this 'could proceed to effect the transition from Capitalism to Socialism with the cooperation of the people'. His other great concern was peacemaking in Europe. He disagreed with the terms of the Treaty of Versailles, which were being imposed on Germany, and wrote a number of articles on the issue. He argued that the economic terms imposed by the victors would make Germany 'an economic slave to other nations'; but, above all, he felt that the settlement was morally unacceptable in that it denied the right of self-determination to many people and would actually make permanent peace unlikely. He reserved especial venom for Lloyd George, the British representative among the 'Big Four' (the Allied Powers). As he wrote in the *Socialist Register*, Lloyd George was 'of all the plenipotentiaries . . . the least fitted for his task. He immerses himself in whatever he has in hand. He is a mere spill on whatever current he happens to float. He has been on both sides of every controversy that has divided the Conference.'

At home, he was concerned about the future of the ILP, some of whose members were keen to link with the forces of international communism via the Third International – a course of action eventually rejected. He remained as treasurer of the Labour Party, but played little part in official Labour business, in spite of the fact that this was a time when Labour was well-poised to supplant the much-weakened Liberals as the main opposition. He despaired of the behaviour and outlook of many members of the party and had little faith in its future. Yet within four years he was to be chosen as its leader, and in January 1924 its first prime minister.

Meanwhile, Labour continued to be ineffective in the House of Commons. Henderson had been re-elected in 1919, but socialists were looking forward to the return of MacDonald and Snowden. MacDonald did himself long-term good by the publicity gained from a by-election in which he stood in Woolwich in 1921. A Unionist who had won the Victoria Cross narrowly defeated him in one of the most vicious campaigns ever known. The intervention of his earlier adversary, Horatio Bottomley, had marked a turning-point, for he declared in *John Bull* that patriotic citizens would have no excuse 'for sending to the House of Commons a man whose war record will stand for all time as a blasphemy on the fair name of Britain'. With other such taunts, with trams running through the constituency bearing posters saying 'A Traitor for Parliament?' and with the 'ruffianism' of Labour supporters against the Coalition candidate backfiring on the Labour standard-bearer, MacDonald's chances were seriously damaged. The dignity of his performance and the small scale of his eventual defeat (by 683 votes) earned him much praise, not only in the country but also among the Labour MPs.

Yet the Woolwich result made it very clear that there were serious obstacles in the path of his political rehabilitation. As the *Evening Standard* put it: 'Woolwich is a Coalition gain. But it is still more a Ramsay MacDonald loss.' This was how the press depicted the outcome, and indeed with some voters there was a problem over his war record. Yet among active members of the party, there was wide recognition of MacDonald's abilities and contribution. It was apparent to many of them that he was a tireless advocate on Labour's behalf, whether speaking from public platforms, writing in the press or producing pamphlets. Indeed, one of the most constructive expositions of Labour policy came from his pen in the 1920 publication, *A Policy for the Labour Party*.

Still on the Executive by virtue of his treasurership, he was nonetheless an irregular attender. At the Annual Conference, he was – according to Beatrice Webb – 'a restless and uneasy spirit'. She noticed how he had distanced himself from the bulk of the party, and that much of his time was spent in the company of ex-Liberals who had joined, rather than with the traditional party regulars. He remained much more committed to the ILP, however, always attended its functions and spent much time in helping to reorganise the organisation. Members were duly grateful, and his principled stand over the war and his activity on their behalf subsequently earned him election to the Executive in 1921. He was, as Austin Morgan remarks, 'ideologically pre-eminent' within the party, and understood its history, traditions and operations better than any contemporary. Such insight enabled him to write his much-praised *History of the ILP*, in 1922.

THE LEADERSHIP CONTEST: MACDONALD VERSUS CLYNES

A general election was called for November 1922, following the fall of the Coalition government. From the Labour point of view, it was a great success, for its membership went up from 57 to 142. The composition of the party at Westminster underwent a profound shift in emphasis, for whereas in the debacle of 1918 only eight of those elected under the party banner had belonged to the ILP or one of the divisional Labour parties, four years later the figures were 32 and 19 respectively. In other words, the influence of the trade unions was weakened overall, and the party acquired a more militant socialist element. Back in Parliament were several of the most well-known pre-war leaders, Fred Jowett, George Lansbury and MacDonald among them, but also elected were many young men who were to play a leading role over the next few decades.

MacDonald's victory in his new Aberavon constituency was a convincing one. The ILP had provided him with strong backing, and he won widespread support from the sort of people he most admired, the ones he described as 'the middle mass of workers, well educated as a rule, religious, interested in the discussion of real issues'. His chairman at that time was Clynes, who had taken over from Adamson in 1921. Clynes quickly antagonised some of the newly-elected members by his failure to win the Speaker's approval for Labour alone to take over the role of the Opposition front bench.

A Parliamentary party meeting was arranged to consider Labour's course of action in the new session. In anticipation of this, an ILP gathering was held at which Emmanuel Shinwell proposed that MacDonald should oppose Clynes for the leadership; only Maxton and Snowden expressed dissent. The PLP meeting was duly held on 21 November 1922, and there was (in MacNeill Weir's words) 'an atmosphere of excitement and expectancy'. Clynes spoke first and explained that although the Speaker was willing to allow PLP leaders to be given precedence over the Liberals in debate, he was not prepared to concede that they should occupy the major portion of the Opposition front bench. Although Clynes expressed his profound dismay at the Speaker's declaration, this was not enough for the newer members. They felt Clynes' tone suggested that he did not regard the matter as very important. As Snowden put it: 'The demeanour of Clynes disappointed the meeting . . . he seemed to have been too easily put off, and to be advising them to accept defeat'.

In a situation where there was obvious disenchantment about the outcome, MacDonald seized his opportunity. He spoke of his dissatisfaction, and successfully urged that a letter be sent to the Speaker to demand exclusive use of the front bench, and those immediately behind. This may have been a calculated ploy to exploit the mood of the meeting, so that a challenge could then be mounted. For when it was proposed that all those officers elected at the end of the last session should continue until the end of the forthcoming one, MacDonald's followers moved that new elections should be held there and then. This was agreed on a show of hands and, in a close contest, the incumbent Clynes was defeated by 61–56. The absence of 22 trade union MPs probably swung the result in MacDonald's favour, an absence which Snowden later recorded was caused by their inability 'to reach the party meeting in time on account of some Trade Union work which detained them'. As a result, he was elected as chairman and leader, with Clynes as his deputy, in the first vote on the chairmanship since 1906.

The choice of titles on this occasion was significant, for it indicated that Labour now accepted its responsibilities as the major Opposition party – and therefore the alternative government should the Conservatives fall. In other words, MacDonald was leader of the Opposition and therefore the potential prime minister.

Why was MacDonald chosen in preference to Clynes?

The details of the meeting as related above are clearly important, for they showed MacDonald to advantage and Clynes to be below par on the big occasion. But it is likely that the plan to bring about his downfall was already carefully laid before the PLP meeting took place. Clynes, not an impartial observer, recalled in his memoirs that the blow had been premeditated. As he put it:

> It is possible that, had I been able to see into the future, I might have taken another line of action in 1922 which would have deprived him of the power to strike . . . when, later, I learned of the complicated plans and schemes made for my defeat, I confess feeling that some of my colleagues had been ungrateful as well as disloyal.

Other sources have verified the claim concerning 'complicated plans and schemes', and in particular Snowden later claimed that MacDonald had been 'actively canvassing among his friends for support, and he had been especially concerned to get the support of the new Scottish members'. The outcome of the ILP meeting suggests that he had some success in this campaign, and although not all of those present favoured his candidature the Clydeside group was committed to him. One of those, David Kirkwood, subsequently described the occasion and the reactions of his colleagues in this way:

> No sooner had we arrived in London than we were plunged into the atmosphere of intrigue. We did not know that atmosphere . . . Now we breathed a new air, the air of intrigue, of personal vanity, of desire for position and power, of suggestion or shrugged shoulders that often conveyed more than words . . . [Having explained that

his fellow Clydesiders were in doubt about who should lead the party, he added] We were Ramsay MacDonald's men. It was the Clyde group of Labour members who made Ramsay MacDonald leader of the Party, and so opened the path to all his future greatness – and failure.

He added that even within the ILP there were differences about whether to nominate MacDonald, but that his own associates in the Clyde group did not have any such doubts. His comments on the anxieties of others present were significant. He quotes Henderson as saying that: 'You Clyde men are determined to put MacDonald in. Well, if you do, it will only be a few years before you are trying to put him out.' Even John Wheatley, a staunchly pro-MacDonald supporter, was shaken by the very obvious hostility to MacDonald, and noted that 'the man seems to have no friends'.

Yet the ILP went ahead with their nomination, for as far as the majority were concerned, MacDonald had proved himself to be a man whose heart was on the left. He had a background of socialist commitment, and his views had been expounded in a plethora of articles and pamphlets, and on the public platform. Above all, his attitude to the war was probably decisive. He had not been seduced by the temptations of office in the Coalition, a point which he was keen to emphasise. In the words of Roy Jenkins in his biography of Attlee, 'they confused pacifism with revolutionary fervour'. As for any suggestions by MacDonald himself that he was not keen to let his name go forward, these were brushed aside as unimportant by men such as Kirkwood '. . . he was always tired. But we knew that he was a terrific worker'.

Other than the Clydesiders and then the ILP as a whole, most of the key figures in the party veered towards Clynes, Snowden and Thomas among them. Snowden, whose comments were often unfavourable towards MacDonald and therefore to be viewed with some scepticism, nonetheless later gave an interesting account of his reasoning. He felt that there were deficiencies in MacDonald's approach, ones which were to be noted by others in the party a decade later. Having said that he favoured allowing Clynes to continue to do the job which he was doing well, he added:

My other objection to Mr MacDonald taking the chair at this time was that I did not think it likely he would give the party a vigorous lead. I had seen a good deal of him in such a position when he was Chairman before the war, and his passion for intrigue and compromise, and his desire to be regarded as a 'gentleman' by the other parties, disqualified him to lead a party which contained so many members who had come into the House of Commons filled with enthusiasm for a fight.

He believed that MacDonald 'played up to the Left Wing, an attitude strikingly different from that he had pursued when in the House of Commons in previous Parliaments'.

There was a further fact which cannot be overlooked, and this was that he looked and sounded the part. Kirkwood noted the obvious comparison: 'Nature had dealt unevenly [with the two contestants]. She had endowed MacDonald with a magnificent presence, a full resonant voice, and a splendid dignity. Clynes was small, unassuming, of uneven features, and voice without colour. There they sat; Clynes at ease and indifferent; MacDonald with his head in his hands, looking drawn, anxious and ill.' He went on to say that once the voting was over and the result announced, there was was huge change in MacDonald's countenance: 'The result acted like magic on MacDonald. He sat up at once. All the lassitude and illness disappeared. He was as vigorous as any man in the room.'

For MacDonald, there was a personal motive in his struggle for the leadership. As he wrote in a letter in 1930, he had stood against Clynes not out of personal ambition but because 'I believed that he & his colleagues had behaved badly to me & because I wanted to avenge the cause of the righteous'. Often MacDonald cast doubt on the motives of those who opposed him, and he tended to see them as involved in conspiratorial or in some way dishonourable behaviour. Victory in 1922 was therefore particularly sweet, for he had routed someone of whose record he disapproved, and he had not expected to win in any case.

What is apparent from the above account is that MacDonald's elevation to the leadership was made possible by the changing character of the Parliamentary Party in which the influence of the trade unionists, still very important, was nonetheless of diminished significance. Against this background, in November 1922 MacDonald outmanoeuvred Clynes very effectively. That he was able to do so owed much to his past record as the man who had suffered for his principles in 1914. His success was also related to the fact that there was no one who could rival him as a convincing leader at a time when the party was on the verge of making a significant breakthrough. As Beatrice Webb put it at the time: 'If he is not the best man for the post, he is at any rate the worst and most dangerous man out of it.' She had her misgivings, but could see that 'looked at impartially, and without considering the way it was done, MacDonald's chairmanship has much to recommend it'. The comment reflects her ambivalent reaction to what had happened. Few could deny MacDonald's credentials, but even among those whose admiration was less qualified some alarm bells occasionally rang. Kirkwood observed that John Wheatley, on seeing MacDonald's changed appearance and demeanour following the declaration of his election as leader, 'looked at me and shrugged his shoulders. His uneasiness was growing'.

timeline	1914	outbreak of First World War; MacDonald resigns chairmanship of PLP over opposition to war
	1915	Labour serves in Asquith Coalition (and in 1916 in Lloyd George one); *John Bull* revelation of his illegitimacy
	1917	two revolutions in Russia (communist one, November 1917); outlines pacifist stand in *National Defence: A Study in Militarism*
	1918	defeated in general election
	1920	writes *A Policy for the Labour Party*
	1922	elected to Westminster again; becomes first leader of Labour Party.

Points to consider

1) Why did MacDonald oppose the First World War?
2) In what ways did he suffer for his opposition to hostilities?
3) Why was MacDonald critical of the performance of the PLP after 1918?
4) Why was Clynes' leadership of the PLP under threat? What assets did MacDonald possess in his challenge to Clynes?

OFFICE AND OPPOSITION, 1924–9

When in October 1922 the Conservatives walked out of the Lloyd George Coalition, the resulting election witnessed the emergence of the Labour Party as the party of alternative government. Labour returned 142 MPs, and secured 4.25 million votes, about a third of the total cast. As the new leader, MacDonald had little time to get the party used to being His Majesty's Opposition, for within a year another snap election was called.

In the early 1920s, there were widely divergent views on tactics within the Labour Party. The ILP was committed to a leftward stance. Under the leadership of Clifford Allen, a man of personal charm and an iron will, there was an inner circle who were committed to the achievement of socialist goals. Fenner Brockway and others did not believe in achieving their objective by force, but by perseverance and courage. MacDonald was still prominent within the ILP, acting as chairman of the information department, and such people presided over an increasing membership as many new branches were opened between 1923–5. The ILP sought to keep Labour on a socialist course, and was an influential group within the party. But many others never shared this concern for the purity of socialist doctrine, and men such as MacDonald and Snowden were committed to moderation. They remained in the ILP even whilst pursuing policies which were unpalatable to its members.

There were annual debates on the meaning of socialism at party conferences, and different characters expounded their differing conceptions of what the term implied and how it should best be achieved. There were also opportunities in Parliament for the meaning of the term to be explored. In March 1923, Philip Snowden initiated a debate on a Private Member's motion, its wording clear: 'In view of the failure of the capitalist system to adequately utilise and organise natural resources and productive power, or to provide the necessary standard of life for the vast numbers of the population, legislative effort should be directed to the gradual supersession of the capitalist system.' The debate attracted much attention at the time.

In April 1923, Labour MPs showed their contempt at the attitude of the Bonar Law Conservative government towards ex-servicemen in the Commons by singing the Red Flag, and precipitating an adjournment of the House. A few years later, one of the ILPers, Jimmy Maxton, infuriated many Conservatives by his attack on the government's parsimony. Because the grant of child-welfare centres was being reduced, the death rate among children was in his view bound to increase: 'In the interests of economy they condemned hundreds of children to death, and I call it murder . . . a cold, callous, deliberate crime in order to save money.' The tumult which followed lasted for over an hour, and *The Times* noted that MacDonald 'sat on the front bench white with anger at the folly of his own supporters'.

Militant demonstrations of this kind illustrated the gulf which was developing within the party between the left and the leadership. MacDonald clearly opposed such displays of fervour. He recognised that Conservatives and Liberals adopted a supercilious attitude to many trade unionists, and a contemptuous one to middle-class socialists whom they considered to be disloyal to people of their own type. He knew how they mocked Sidney Webb with the shout of 'sit down, Nanny,' because his beard was thought to bear a passing resemblance to that of a goat. But by their outbursts and by the policies they pursued, they exacerbated the tension which was always there anyway. To MacDonald, if Labour was to succeed as being more than a party of and for the working classes, it needed to earn respect, and he felt that members had to rise above the disdainful way in which they were sometimes themselves treated, and demonstrate their own sense of responsibility.

Even the most zealous socialists could sometimes accommodate themselves to their new surroundings surprisingly well. They were liable to be seduced by the atmosphere and conventions of the House, and if some members on the government side were condescending and rude, others proffered the hand of friendship. Some were tolerant and well-disposed, Baldwin among them. The alliance of Baldwin and MacDonald, which was to dominate the next decade, was based on mutual goodwill and forbearance. There were other Conservatives who even invited Clydesiders to their weekend parties. It was the same David Kirkwood who so disappoved of the pomp and formality of the State Opening of Parliament who was later to record that: 'I had to shake myself occasionally, as I found myself moving about and talking with men whose names were household words. More strange was it to find them all so simple and unaffected, and friendly'. For MacDonald it was easy to become absorbed into such an atmosphere, and from an early stage after his return he established political and social ties with members on all sides.

In the election which Baldwin called in December 1923 Labour made substantial gains. Even among Conservatives there was much unease about the government's decision to fight a campaign on the issue of protection. The decision helped to reunite the divided Liberals, for they had a long tradition of support for Free Trade. Labour also opposed tariffs as a solution to unemployment and entered the contest in good heart. Having hurriedly adopted many candidates in vacant seats, it polled well, securing 4 438 000 votes. It won 191 seats, an improvement of 49, with the Conservatives being still the largest party (258 seats, down from 346) but now without an absolute majority. The Liberals were pushed into third place.

Much depended on the attitude of the Liberals. In the uncertain parliamentary situation, Baldwin held on until Parliament reassembled in January 1924, and in that interlude the Liberals were inundated with requests to save the country from the perceived socialist threat. The City of London was alarmed at the prospect a Labour government might hold for sterling; others feared that Labour would undermine national defence. Mowat recorded one of the stranger concerns: 'Some [even] professed to believe that under Labour the marriage tie would not be sacred and that free love would receive official sanction'. The *English Review* was prompted to say: 'For the first time in her history the party of revolution approach their hands to the helm of state . . . with the design of destroying the very basis of civilised life'. Churchill detected a particular threat:

> The enthronement in office of a Socialist Government will be a serious national misfortune such as has usually befallen great

states only on the morrow of defeat in war. It will delay the return of prosperity, it will open a period of increasing political confusion and disturbance, it will place both the Liberal and Labour parties in a thoroughly false position ... Strife and tumults, deepening and darkening, will be the only consequence of minority Socialist rule.

In spite of such alarm, Asquith felt that Labour should be given its opportunity. Apart from its electoral strength as recently demonstrated, there was another, more self-interested consideration. Any tactical Conservative–Liberal alliance to exclude it from power would serve to strengthen it in the future. This was the best time to allow an experiment with Labour, a point which Neville Chamberlain accepted. In office, he felt, Labour 'would be too weak to do much harm, but not too weak to get discredited'.

Labour saw its chance, for although it would be in office without power, few wanted to pass over the opportunity. Even many of the Clydesiders and the ILP were in favour of Labour forming a ministry. They wanted the party to enter government and present the House with a challenging socialist programme. If the opposing parties united in horror to defeat them, they felt that Labour would receive the backing of the country in a resulting election. MacDonald, Snowden, Henderson and other leading figures also wanted office, but by temperament and inclination they were not the men to challenge the Conservatives and Liberals. Snowden records that MacDonald was initially doubtful about the wisdom of having 'office without power', but other authorities detected a strong impression that despite his understandable reservations he was keen to be Prime Minister.

He may, of course, have lamented the lack of talent and experience in the party hierarchy to fill offices of government, and have felt that the demands of the left would make his task a difficult one. But two factors over all other considerations inclined MacDonald to accept. It would be cowardly and foolish to forsake an opportunity to carry out at least some part of Labour policy in the domestic and overseas sphere. Moreover, whatever happened – even if the government was unable to accomplish very much in its dependent position – it would have shown that it could and was willing to take over. He believed that Labour must accept the offer, for to refuse would suggest that Labour was unready then or even in the foreseeable future to assume the reins of office. As he put it: 'If we shirk our responsibilities now we should inflict upon ourselves the defeat our enemies could not inflict upon us'. Hence his speech at Hull: 'One step! ... on one condition that it leads to the next step'.

It was, then, with the full consent of most of his colleagues and in line with his own wishes, that he became Prime Minister. He recognised the difficulties of the situation and described it as 'what we must all admit will be a task of almost incalculable magnitude'. Even to him, it was an 'insane miracle' that Labour should be poised for office. But having got into such a position, he was certainly not sympathetic to the view of the left that the purpose of assuming office was to produce a challenging socialist programme which could then be put before the voters. He felt that it would be fatuous to 'go in for the sake of coming out', for this would have thrown away the chance of persuading the vast non-socialist element in the electorate that Labour was serious about placing the national interest above party advantage. Above all, he wanted to win the confidence of such people, and therefore it would be essential to administer the nation's affairs in a responsible manner.

MacDonald was ready when on 21 January the Government was beaten on an Opposition amendment to the King's Speech. Baldwin resigned and MacDonald was asked by George V to head a Labour administration. There was much enthusiasm within the Labour Movement for the decision, whatever happened thereafter.

MacDonald personally seemed well-suited for the task, for although he lacked ministerial experience he had demonstrated his abilities in a variety of administrative tasks within the party and the wider Movement, and his abilities as a skilled negotiator and in balancing the different factions within his party were widely recognised. He had written widely on socialism and labour matters, he knew more about foreign affairs than most other Labour members and, as a prolific journalist, his writings were known to a wider audience.

CABINET-MAKING

For all of the fears about what a Labour government might involve, there was in truth little reason for alarm. Some of the proposals for more radical ideas, such as nationalisation and a capital levy, had been embraced by people not members of the Labour Movement; but in any case, given the Parliamentary arithmetic, there was little likelihood that they could be carried out. Above all, MacDonald was an adherent of gradualism, and at his party's victory celebration his remark on the need for one step at a time suggested that he was not a man about to embark upon an adventurously challenging programme. He saw the limits of manoeuvre open to him, and was more than ready to adapt to the situation he confronted. There were many around him who, whatever their past rhetoric, were no enthusiasts for an immediate effort to nationalise the means of production, distribution and exchange.

Over Christmas 1923 MacDonald had contemplated the creation of the first Labour Cabinet in British history, only corresponding with Henderson during his self-imposed isolation in his beloved Lossiemouth. However, relations with Henderson had always been strained, and at first he was tempted to exclude him or give him a lowly position, an odd decision bearing in mind the long services which he had given the party and his previous ministerial experience. MacDonald and Henderson never got on well together, for their personalities and their approach to political issues were very different. Malcolm Muggeridge (*The Thirties*), a writer who observed both men from close quarters, provided us with a portrait of their contrasting natures:

> Henderson, a regular chapel-goer and occasional lay-preacher, extremely respectable, with bowler hat and umbrella, was suspicious of MacDonald's marked liking for the company of his social superiors; MacDonald considered Henderson commonplace and lower middle class . . . They represented two elements in the Labour Party.

Whatever MacDonald's preferences, it would have been remarkable if such personal considerations had been allowed to dictate the composition of the ministry. One of the main difficulties of the would-be Prime Minister in Cabinet-making was that he faced a situation in which so few of his colleagues had any governmental or administrative experience. But of those who were eminent within the Movement, in several cases he took a pessimistic view of their potential.

In the days before the government's inevitable defeat, MacDonald was in touch with several prominent men outside the party who had exhibited a broadly sympathetic attitude to the left. By so doing he might be able to include at least some persons with ministerial experience. In some cases such people were given a 'technical' office, such as the Admiralty; others, including prominent ex-Liberals, were put into more senior positions. Charles Trevelyan was given responsibility for education and Lord Haldane became Lord Chancellor. Three Cabinet members had been left-wing Liberals MPs prior to 1914, and Sidney Webb was also an ex-Liberal.

The difficulty was in filling posts in the Upper House, for this was a chamber in which Labour was unrecognised. Five peers were eventually found and they were to prove appropriate for their task, but with one exception they were not really Labour appointees. Otherwise it was a question of allocating the leading party personnel to key governmental offices and filling the rest with less well-known figures. According to J. H. Thomas, the rail leader, there was some doubt as to what appointments were necessary, and the leaders had to seek out an almanack to ascertain the list of offices which had to be filled.

In the event, Henderson got the Home Office, Snowden the Treasury, and MacDonald served as his own Foreign Secretary ('I determined to take on my back a double burden, not that I was unmindful of the weakness of human flesh, but I was convinced that, if our country was to pull its full weight, the authority of the Premiership would have to be cast into the same scale as that of the Foreign Secretaryship'). Key posts were thus filled with moderates from the middle classes, some of whom were relatively new to the party. Only five trade unionists were included in the Cabinet, and only two left-wing figures – the Catholic businessman and Clydesider, John Wheatley, who became Minister of Health, and Fred Jowett, an ILP member of an older generation of socialists, who became Minister of Works. Yet it was a very different Cabinet from the ones that had gone before, and 11 came from the working class, many with a background in the union movement. It marked a social revolution, despite its moderation; working men were in a majority, the great public schools and the old universities being eclipsed for the first time. Only two had ever sat in a Cabinet before, Haldane and Henderson, and 15 of the 20 had never had a ministerial post of any kind. As A. J. P. Taylor observes:

'Inevitably, they relied on the civil servants in their departments and these, though personally sympathetic, were not running over with enthusiasm for an extensive socialist programme'.

The composition of the party was reassuring to outside opinion, and the presence of men such as the ex-Liberal Lord Haldane as Lord Chancellor helped to reassure Westminster opinion and the general public at large. Yet MacDonald needed few lessons in the need for moderation, and could accept the King's advice to employ 'prudence and sagacity' without any ill-will.

Members of the government were required to take up their seals of office and this involved a visit to Buckingham Palace to see the King. Some ministers possessed no formal dress and on this occasion paraded in their ordinary attire. MacDonald was later to insist on formal dress for formal occasions, and three sets of appropriate court clothing were obtained for use by ministers as necessary. The matter had symbolic significance, for it showed that the Prime Minister was keen to demonstrate that Labour could be trusted and that a Labour government would not mark too radical a departure from tradition. This would be the more easy to do if ministers 'looked the part'. To others, such compliance with traditional practice was a sign that Labour was selling out to its class enemies, and they felt that MacDonald was being excessively mild and timid in his approach. Many also suggested that personal vanity was a factor, that he felt he looked especially imposing in court dress, wearing his silver-buckled shoes and sword.

George V soon put ministers at ease by what seemed to be a genuine friendliness. He was disposed to give Labour the benefit of the doubt. As he later told his mother, 'They [the new ministers] have different ideas to ours as they are all socialists, but they ought to be given a chance and ought to be treated fairly.' On the day MacDonald and the others kissed his hand, he recorded in his diary: 'I had an hour's talk with him; he impressed me very much; he wishes to do the right thing. Today, 23 years ago, dear Grandmama died. I wonder what she would have thought of a Labour government!'

To party members in the country, tales of ministers wearing formal dress and receiving coaching in court etiquette were deeply perturbing. They did not expect their representatives to continue with such outdated traditions, hence the frustration of the shipyard workers who

MacDonald and the trappings of power; in court dress

at one gathering cried out: 'A workers' government, ye ca' it! It's a bloody lum hat government like a' the rest'.

Others disagreed, and some of those who served interpreted the arrival of the party in office differently. They recognised the startling nature of the party's advance. It was Clynes who later wrote of his feelings in this way:

> As we stood waiting for his Majesty, amid the gold and crimson of the Palace, I could not help marvelling at the strange turn of Fortune's wheel, which had brought MacDonald the starveling clerk, Thomas the engine driver, Henderson the foundry labourer and Clynes the mill-hand to this pinnacle.

Such a comment indicates that far from contemplating a revolution as the *English Review* had feared, leaders were overawed by a system which, as Thomas marvelled, 'enables the engine driver of yesterday to be the minister of today'.

MacDonald was in no doubt of the importance of reassuring public opinion. As he wrote to Lord Parmoor, an ex-Tory, devout Churchman and eccelsiastical lawyer, and also a relative of Beatrice Webb, his aim was 'to gain the confidence of the country'. He recognised that in many ways Labour was unready for office and that if it could establish a reputation for competence then it would have achieved something worthwhile.

He was in any case not disposed to experiments in socialism. The parliamentary situation suited him rather well, for dependence on the Liberals gave him a reason for pursuing the path of moderation and responsibility. Committed socialists realised that he was only too willing to hide behind his minority status as an excuse for inaction, and felt that he did not listen to the views of his supporters nor to those of the trade unions. They disliked this tame approach, and felt that he had lost touch with them. It was the secretary of the Parliamentary ILP, Fenner Brockway, who later recorded an incident which served to confirm their suspicions. On seeing his fellow MP, MacDonald, who was attired in evening dress, enquired: 'Well, Fenner, what commands have you brought me today?' He then quickly gave an important prime ministerial function as his reason for having 'no time to listen to the views of the Group'.

MacDonald quickly established an overwhelming ascendancy in the

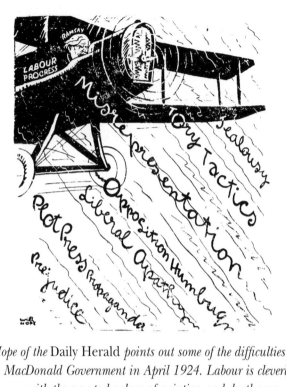

Will Hope of the Daily Herald *points out some of the difficulties facing the minority MacDonald Government in April 1924. Labour is cleverly associated with the new technology of aviation and death-rays*

party, partly as a result of the numerous offices he held. Not only was he Prime Minister and Foreign Secretary, but outside Parliament he was still treasurer and, as it happened, chairman of Labour's National Executive Committee for the year 1923–4. The predominance he exercised was soon apparent, and Beatrice Webb could write to her husband (President of the Board of Trade) that 'he [MacDonald] is head and shoulders above the rest of the Cabinet'. Indeed, not only was he supreme, he was also in her view becoming increasingly aloof and remote, to the point of being high-handed in his treatment of those around him. From an early stage there was tension in the relationship between the government and its supporters in and out of Parliament, and the latter in particular felt that their views were ignored.

LABOUR IN OFFICE: DOMESTIC POLICY

Even in the view of its moderate supporters, the first Labour government, relying as it did on Liberal support for its existence, achieved little. Having eschewed the bold approach favoured by the ILP and other socialist societies, it was on the defensive. By comparison, a bolder approach might have put the Liberals on the defensive. There were modest changes which made life more tolerable for working people. There was some easing of the conditions applying to unemployment benefit. The gap between benefit periods under unemployment insurance arrangements was abolished, and in another measure benefits were increased and uncovenanted ones (beyond those covered by insurance) were made a statutory right rather than a discretionary grant. Whereas previously applicants had been interrogated by officials in the unemployment bureau (the labour exchange) and were dependent on their generosity, the attitude changed. In the 1924 election young males were known to shout out 'Vote Labour – and be treated like a gentleman at the bureau'. The limit on the private means of pensioners, if derived from savings rather than earnings, was raised. Country Agricultural Wage Committees were established to fix minimum wages within their areas of jurisdiction.

At education, some of the cheese-paring economies of the Geddes 'Axe' of 1922 were eased. The effectiveness of the ambitious Fisher Act of 1918 had been undermined by the post-war search for retrenchment, and so instead of expansion in educational provision there had been a standstill. Trevelyan, capable and progressive, was able to make funds available for an increase in the number of free places in secondary schools and to revive state scholarships to university. A survey of obsolete school buildings was put in hand, and 40 was set as the maximum class size in elementary schools. With encouragement given to proposals for raising the leaving age to 15 and the provision of adult learning opportunities, the Board of Education became what C. Brand, a historian of the Labour Movement, has described as 'the patron of progressive local authorities rather than an agent of financial restriction'.

What Trevelyan had, and many other ministers lacked, was a clear programme for action. R. H. Tawney, a prominent Labour thinker of the era, had drafted a statement of Labour policy, *Secondary Education for All*, and for several years this was to be the basis of Labour thinking and action on educational issues. It was Trevelyan who established a committee under Sir Henry Hadow to report on the further needs of education. Although the Hadow Report (which established the break between the primary and the secondary school at the age of 11) did not apppear until 1926, when Labour was out of office, it reflected in the main the policies advocated by Trevelyan.

At the Exchequer, Snowden was a pillar of Gladstonian orthodoxy, his language replete with considerations of financial rectitude. It was difficult to embark on any innovative or expansionary schemes, and although he gave general support for various public works programmes involving roadbuilding and municipal tasks, this was only on the condition that they did not threaten to produce an imbalance in the national finances. In his budget, he used the surplus of revenue over expenditure to reduce duties on imported food and repeal the McKenna duties, and this was a considerable move towards free trade. This meant that the 'free breakfast table' was brought nearly into being, in that duties on such things as cocoa, coffee, sugar and tea were much reduced.

One measure stood out. Wheatley had responsibility for housing, and the Clydesider was the most advanced socialist in the ministerial team. He combined Catholicism and political radicalism, and under his control the Ministry of Health became largely a ministry of housing. His Housing Act enabled the Government to subsidise to the tune of £9 per house annually for 40 years the building of over 500 000 council houses. The scheme was eventually dropped in 1933 but by then it had made a significant impact on the housing situation. His other proposal, agreed with the building unions, to increase the number of apprentices in the trade, helped to secure the labour force needed to produce the extended programme, and had the benefit of helping young men acquire some useful skills, the first example of such cooperation of government and industry in peacetime. It was an effective approach, based upon the recognition that there was a long-term housing shortage. Most MPs agreed that there was a problem of housing provision, and although the bill had a long and difficult passage its underlying principle that housing provision was a social obligation gained wide assent. The achievement was all the more remarkable, for Wheatley was operating in an area where there was no plan of action.

Labour enthusiasts might agree that poor living conditions were repugnant, but they had not previously discussed how the long-term problems might be tackled. If the measure did nothing for those who lacked any accommodation and failed to remove the slums, it was nonethless a breakthough.

DISILLUSION IN THE PARTY

Despite the Wheatley measure, there was regular sniping from the left of the party and from the disunited Liberals who could agree only on their criticism of the Government's inability to tackle unemployment. It was an easy target, for in truth although Labour supporters might claim to care more about the topic than did their opponents – probably with some justification – there were no clear proposals in mind and Snowden's financial orthodoxy ruled out any prospect of innovative schemes. Adelman puts it rather well in *The Rise and Fall of the Labour Party, 1880–1945* (Longman, 1972), when he claims that:

> The Labour Party seemed hypnotised by the belief that in the long run, with the introduction of socialism, the problem of unemployment would disappear. In the short run . . . apart from paying lip-service to the notion of public works, which were often costly and slow to take effect, it was rather helpless before the complexities of the problem. Over unemployment, the party leadership in 1924 was timid, unconstructive and muddled in its thinking, though in this it was partly the victim of the conventional economic wisdom of the time. The seeds were already being sown for the disaster that was to overtake it in 1931.

The Conservatives kept up a constant harassment, as would be expected in such a parliamentary situation. Not surprisingly, the life expectancy of the government was constantly in peril, but MacDonald made it clear from the outset that minor defeats would be no cause for resignation. There were several adverse votes, but the government survived them and was eventually to succumb over a more controversial episode, relations with the Soviet Union. To the work of the MacDonald administration in foreign policy we must now turn.

FOREIGN POLICY

MacDonald, personally in charge at the Foreign Office, acquired a deserved reputation as a world peacemaker. He took over at a time when there was a clear opportunity to improve Britain's relationship with its European neighbours, and his Gladstonian principles of seeking to resolve problems by peaceful and reasonable means were appropriate and made good sense. The Cabinet backed him in the knowledge that such an approach would win the approval of the Liberals and help to convince them that they had been wise to entrust Labour with office.

In personal terms, MacDonald was well-equipped for the handling of foreign policy. His easy charm and good grace were assets as he presided over international gatherings, and whereas his party colleagues often found him distant and aloof such qualities were not apparent when he was in the company of world statesmen. He ensured that he was informed about their attitudes and inclinations, and was prepared to work diligently to familiarise himself with the detail of the issues involved. Moreover, he had definite priorities, among which was a desire to 'open up' diplomacy and change the atmosphere in which relations with other countries were conducted. He soon told the House that it would be shown all treaty details, and as a gesture of goodwill he made available all background papers concerned with the events which had led up to the outbreak of war in 1914 – long before the then customary lapse of 50 years prior to release.

His party had always proclaimed its commitment to international peace. It had condemned the Treaty of Versailles as excessively punitive, and it similarly criticised Britain's inaction over the French invasion of the Ruhr in January 1923 which had damaged relations between Paris and London. Harold Nicolson, a historian and politician well-versed in the diplomatic scene, later wrote of MacDonald's priorities on assuming responsibility for handling the aftermath of these events:

> [He] wished to re-establish relations of confidence and cooperation with France and Italy; to break the deadlock over reparations; to secure a French evacuation of the Rhineland; and to re-introduce Germany in to the community of nations. He

wished to further the cause of general disarmament by strengthening the machinery of international arbitration; and to bridge the gulf that, both politically and financially, sundered Great Britain from Soviet Russia. Within the space of eight months, he was able either to attain or promote all these seven objects.

There were three dominant areas of policy with which we should concern ourselves: reparations, developments in the League of Nations, and relations with Russia. Much of this work was dealt with effectively and successfully, even if the cost to MacDonald's health of his dual responsibility was considerable. He must be given much of the credit for what went well, although equally he was substantially to blame for the one area of policy in which the government's record was weak and open to criticism, the relationship with the Soviet Union.

The Reparations Issue

Already, the Foreign Office under Lord Curzon's direction had begun to improve relations with the French Government, and MacDonald was personally well-suited to continue the task. Britain was unhappy about the French desire to ruin Germany via its occupation, and he addressed their spokesmen with a mixture of personal goodwill backed by firm disapproval of French behaviour. At an early stage, he wrote to Poincaré, the French premier, in friendly terms, expressing the hope that 'by the strenuous action of good will' it would 'be possible to promote peace and security in Europe'. Poincaré responded with similarly gracious words, and the reply encouraged the British Prime Minister to move on to more concrete issues.

Some Frenchmen were already wondering whether the occupation of the Ruhr would produce any beneficial outcome, and there were Germans who realised that resistance to the occupation and the high inflation that accompanied it were not in Germany's longer-term interests. The time was ripe for pacification, for there seemed to be some reason to hope for a measure of Franco-German reconciliation. The publication of the Dawes Report in April 1924 provided a basis for German repayment of its reparations debt, via an international loan. Also, the replacement of Poincaré by the radical and more amenable

Edouard Herriot made French acceptance of the plan easier than it might have been otherwise, for the new leader had not been involved in the French invasion of the Ruhr which had provoked the rift between Britain and France. A conference was therefore summoned in London in July to settle arrangements, and representatives from Belgium, France, Italy, Japan, the USA and other nations arrived. The French right was concerned that the Treaty of Versailles might be undermined, but MacDonald was able to ease anxieties in a preliminary visit to Paris.

He chaired the London Conference and, as soon as there was the basis of an agreement, the German government was invited to send delegates. After difficult negotiations involving Herriot and the German internationalist, Gustav Stresemann, agreement was reached on evacuation of the Ruhr. MacDonald had handled the situation effectively, presiding over the assembled delegates with tact and skill, and impressing everyone with his capacity for hard work and his mastery of the issues involved. He looked the part and was convincing in his role as an international statesman and mediator. Moreover, in bilateral discussion and small committees, his manner was soothing, calming storms as they arose, and he was largely responsible for establishing more cordial relations between the French and German negotiators. For MacDonald, the Conference and settlement were, in Professor Lyman's words, 'the high point of his career'. It was with a feeling of relief that the issue of reparations had been brought to an end. In MacDonald's phrase, 'we sign it [the agreement] with a feeling that we have turned our backs on the terrible years of war and war mentality'.

The League of Nations

Labour had always supported the League of Nations, and the 1923 manifesto had spelt out its commitment to 'a policy of international cooperation through a strengthened and enlarged League of Nations; the settlement of disputes by conciliation and judicial arbitration . . . [and] Disarmament, the only security for the nations'. Lord Parmoor was given a special responsibility for League affairs and his reputation both as a pacifist and a supporter of the new machinery was an encouragement to those who looked for a conciliatory approach in international affairs.

In September 1924, a high-powered delegation attended the annual Assembly of the League in Geneva, including MacDonald, Parmoor and Henderson. MacDonald stressed the importance of arbitration in international disputes, and the British team was much involved in devising the Protocol for the Pacific Settlement of International Disputes, better known as the Geneva Protocol. The Protocol was unanimously adopted in October 1924, and it tied security to disarmament. It provided for a disarmament conference the following year and the means of resolving tension through the Permanent Court of International Justice or via the use of an appointed arbitrator. If a peaceful resolution of any dispute was not possible, then the Council of the League could eventually call upon member states to apply sanctions. The Labour Party was officially committed to ratification, but the next Conservative government killed the Protocol.

MacDonald was thereby spared the necessity of signing a document about which he had reservations. His primary interest was disarmament and he noted the French view that their negotiators had secured the concession that their security could ultimately be guaranteed by force. He was committed to arrangements to prevent war, but disliked the employment of coercion in international affairs, even by economic sanctions. Whether Labour would have finally accepted the document is a matter of conjecture. Before he left Geneva, MacDonald told Parmoor not to sign immediately, but this may have been because he wished to insert more reservations into the final version.

Relations with Russia

It was the attempt of the MacDonald government to make friendly overtures to the Soviet Union which led to its downfall. MacDonald was determined to normalise relations between Britain and Russia. In March 1921 a trade agreement had been signed but following that relations had markedly deteriorated. Anti-British propaganda regularly appeared in Russia, two British subjects were killed and Lord Curzon had in May 1923 sent a stern note of rebuke. Many British politicians, even those of a more moderate hue such as Baldwin, shared in a general distaste for and suspicion of the USSR, and among the more partisan Conservatives the rhetoric used in denunciations of Bolshevism was often lurid and alarmist. Churchill's concluding words in *The*

Aftermath are an illustration of this near-hysteria: 'Russia, self-outcast, sharpens her bayonets in her Arctic night, and mechanically proclaims through half-starved lips her philosophy of hatred and death'.

Against this unpromising background, MacDonald acted with what might seem to be courage or foolishness, according to personal viewpoint. He announced British *de jure* (legal) recognition of the Soviet government as a legal entity in February, and thereby resumed diplomatic relations. Its representatives were invited to a London conference in April to resolve contentious matters between the two countries. There was an unhappy background chorus of press attacks on Britain in Moscow, and the negotiations in London became deadlocked, reopening in August. They soon broke down again, over the claims of British subjects living in pre-revolutionary Russia. Some Britons had suffered losses because of Russia's seizure of property and default on bonds.

In these inauspicious circumstances, left-wing Labour members acted as intermediaries between Rakovsky (the Soviet chargé d'affaires in London) and Arthur Ponsonby (the under-secretary for foreign affairs), and an agreement was eventually reached. Two treaties were drawn up, a commercial one granting most-favoured-nation privileges for members of the Russian trade delegation, and a general one for later negotiation concerning property confiscated from British residents and the payment of pre-revolutionary debts. In return for a resolution of the dispute, Britain would offer a loan to the Soviet government. There were expressions of mutual goodwill, of willingness to live in peace and friendship, and to refrain from propaganda and other actions which might threaten to damage the relationship.

The storm over the treaties raged furiously, for this was an issue which offered clear scope for opponents seeking partisan advantage. Liberals and Conservatives were very hostile to the treaty and to the proposed loan in particular, for they saw the latter as a means of strengthening the forces of the Communist International which they wanted to see undermined rather than supported. In the Conservative *Morning Post* the attack was taken up with relish. Politicians and businessmen echoed the cry, and by the autumn the days of the government were looking numbered as Liberal support could no longer be taken for granted. MacDonald postponed ratification of the treaties until after the recess.

DECLINE AND DEATH OF THE ADMINISTRATION

The government had made a worthwhile effort to improve relations with the Soviet Union, although the handling of the endeavour – particularly seen in retrospect – is open to criticism. The initial timing of the overtures to Moscow seemed precipitate in the eyes of even some members of the Labour Party, for there had been little sign of goodwill towards Britain. Any attempt at improving the climate was likely to be portrayed as being 'soft on communism'. But whatever doubts there may be over the details of the policy adopted towards Russia, this should not detract from the successes in other areas of diplomacy. A Conservative critic, J. L. Garvin, summarised Labour's performance in *The Observer*, in August 1924:

> Mr MacDonald has largely succeeded in restoring confidence to Anglo-French relations; he has brought Germany into negotiation on an equality; he has helped to bring the reparations question within sight of a genuine solution for the first time . . . and he has followed recognition of the Russian Government by the treaty signed last week. Labour can claim that it has made a mark upon the foreign policy of the country.

Indeed, in the autumn of that year, ministers enjoyed a high level of public support, and outside the party there were other commentators willing to concede that Labour had demonstrated that it was able to govern. However, it was not long before compliments gave way to criticism, and the last months of the Labour government were uninspiring even for the most sympathetic observers to behold.

Before the government could be defeated over ratification of the Russian treaties, it was brought down by what seemed to be a relatively trivial incident. In a communist magazine with only a limited circulation, the *Workers' Weekly*, an article was published which incited British troops to mutiny. It called on soldiers not to shoot their working-class comrades during any industrial or military warfare. The Director of Public Prosecutions decided to prosecute the acting-editor, J. R. Campbell, for sedition, but on the decision of the Attorney-General, Sir Patrick Hastings, the prosecution was withdrawn during the parliamentary recess. He suggested that there was a lack of conclusive evidence, and that no jury would convict in such circumstances. There may have been other motives. Campbell had volunteered for military service in 1914, and was a cripple as a result of his wartime injuries. He had been decorated for exceptional gallantry, and this aroused a certain sympathy for him. In any case the prosecution could have been interpreted as an infringement of the right of free speech.

Party opponents saw things differently, and decided that the case had been withdrawn because of the attitude of Labour backbenchers. The Establishment scented left-wing interference with the judicial process, arguing that outside forces were being allowed to deflect the course of justice in British courts. They argued that favouritism had been shown to the accused, and they moved a vote of censure in the House. Although the Liberals were active in seeking to avoid such a move and suggested that a House committee should examine the issue, MacDonald was unwilling to let the decisions of ministers be so referred for consideration. MacDonald let it be known that if a Liberal amendment to the motion was carried, the defeat would be regarded as a vote of censure on the government. The amendment was carried, and the Prime Minister asked for a dissolution.

He and Hastings had not handled the situation with much skill, and whereas at least the latter had answered the charges in the House in October with some dexterity MacDonald was less convincing. His own speech did more to obscure than to clarify the events, and his argument that he had been too immersed in issues of foreign policy to have kept the matter in sharp focus seemed merely to indicate that he was unfit to carry such a heavy double responsibility. Ministers were not yet finished with the public hysteria caused by the 'red' bogey.

One other incident caused much unease, particularly among Labour supporters. The reputation of MacDonald was tarnished by suggestions of financial impropriety. In September 1924, the *Daily Mail* discovered that he had been allocated £30 000-worth of preference shares by a Scottish biscuit company. Shortly afterwards, the controlling member of the company, Sir Alexander Grant, had received a baronetcy 'for public services'. Whilst still Prime Minister, MacDonald had argued that the shares were to cover the running costs of a Daimler motor car with which the businessman had presented him, and the allotment of the shares was a feature of a very old friendship dating back to childhood days in Morayshire – a story confirmed by Grant.

Many were unconvinced by MacDonald's defence, and there was

scathing comment in left-wing circles about this need to ride in a lordly motor car, though his immediate colleagues seemed much less concerned. They felt that Sir Alexander had deserved his award for his generous endowment of public libraries and other philanthropic contributions to the welfare of the working classes, and believed that he had been genuinely troubled by the indignity of a Prime Minister who lacked appropriate transport from his house in North London to 10 Downing Street. Others were less impressed, and saw the episode as further evidence of MacDonald's doubtful commitment to the socialist cause.

At the end of 1924 the car and the shares were returned to Grant. The issue was largely exhausted by the time of the election, although in MacDonald's own contest in Aberavon the matter was raised by his opponents who found it an ideal issue to exploit. 'Biscuits' was shouted at him as he addressed lively election meetings.

THE 1924 ELECTION

When MacDonald addressed the Annual Conference in October 1924, he was rapturously received. He was given a fulsome tribute which ended in these words: 'We place on record our appreciation of the service he has devoted to the Party, and express our hearty confidence in his leadership'. The motion of congratulation was passed without any discussion and carried unanimously and with thunderous applause. When he announced at the end of the Conference that there was to be an election, he received what the Conference Report called 'a tumultuous ovation'.

The manner of departure may have left ministers with little glory, yet Labour was in optimistic mood once the election was announced. By-election results had been generally encouraging for the government, and the manifesto *Labour's Appeal to the People* was one on which many members thought they could win. It stressed the pre-eminent need to secure international peace and proudly listed what had been done to promote it.

In the election campaign, the party leaders broadcast to the nation for the first time. Baldwin was quietly effective in his use of the microphone, and by comparison MacDonald seemed ranting. His attack on the opposition parties which had turned out the government was not a great success. In their propaganda, the Conservatives and Liberals united in their condemnation of socialism and the Russian treaty. One leaflet even suggested that home, family and religion were all at stake. In some cases Liberal candidates stood down, and the party backed its erstwhile rivals in an anti-socialist stand.

The press also did much to encourage Russophobia, and in the final week the tone of the campaign it conducted became more hostile. Headlines in *The Times* included 'Red Danger in Britain', and 'A Bankrupt Party', and there were various election stunts to discredit the government. Then four days before polling came the bombshell, when the *Daily Mail* announced a 'Soviet Plot', and ran the story of 'Red Propaganda in Britain. Revolution urged by Zinoviev'. This was the matter of the notorious Zinoviev Letter, the best-known of all pre-election scares.

The Zinoviev Letter

The letter purported to be a secret communication from the president of the Third Communist International in Moscow to the small British Communist Party, but it fell into the hands of the Foreign Office. It urged British communists to seek ratification of the Russian treaties, and contained information on the ways by which communism might be spread in Britain. It showed how to prepare the working classes for military insurrection, and included such warning passages as:

Armed warfare must be preceded by a struggle against the inclinations to compromise which are embedded among the majority of British workmen, against the idea of evolution and peaceful extermination of capitalism.

It went on to recommend that cells of communist adherents be established in key places of work and in the army, so that if war broke out 'it is possible to paralyse all the military preparations of the bourgeoisie and make a start in turning an imperialist war into a class war'.

The temperature of the election campaign immediately soared, for in the eyes of Conservative leaders and supporters it was further evidence of the 'red peril' that threatened Britain. They used the letter

ON THE LOAN TRAIL.

[In a document just disclosed by the British Foreign Office (apparently after considerable delay), M. ZINOVIEFF, a member of the Bolshevist Dictatorship, urges the British Communist Party to use "the greatest possible energy" in securing the ratification of Mr. MACDONALD's Anglo-Russian Treaty, in order to facilitate a scheme for "an armed insurrection" of the British proletariat.]

This Punch *illustration (October 1924) by the pro-Conservative cartoonist, Partridge, shows the popular association between Labour and the Bolsheviks; a vote for Labour was seen by some contemporaries as a vote for the beastly and dangerous 'Reds'* to back up their allegation that socialism and communism were inextricably linked, and warned that Labour was too closely associated with Moscow and within its ranks contained dangerous 'fellow-travellers'.

Labour was caught in a quandary, and candidates looked for leadership to MacDonald. They got very little, certainly not the strong and clear statement they hoped for. He had been expecting a pre-election stunt and asked the Foreign Office to investigate the authenticity of the document as soon as it was received. He requested officials to draw up an official protest to the Soviet regime which could be published, but this did not reach him for several days as he was on the campaign trail. When the Foreign Office realised that the *Mail* was about to publish, it quickly issued its protest note, and the Russian government responded with a denial of any knowledge of the document. But not until 27 October, just two days before the election, did the Prime Minister make his statement, in which he denounced the episode as a 'political plot'.

Again, the handling of the affair seemed to have been bungled, for although he suspected at an early stage that the letter was a forgery MacDonald did not express his view with sufficient speed. Officials in Whitehall may have let him down, but he did not seem to sense the urgency of a rebuttal. The *Manchester Guardian* noted his 'attitude of unruffled aloofness', and the paper which had published the letter assumed that his failure to speak out sooner was an indication of his wish 'to deceive the British people . . . everyone would have expected our Socialist Ministers to reply by expelling every Bolshevik in Britain.' When MacDonald's public comment was made at a speech in Cardiff, it was inadequate for the situation, and as was often the case it raised more issues than it clarified. Not surprisingly, some members of the Cabinet could see the dangers of the situation more clearly; 'we're bunkered', lamented Thomas.

For years the authenticity of the document has been debated. Labour was convinced that it was a forgery to frighten off potential voters, and the general consensus is that it was. It was probably concocted by White Russian émigrés, with members of the security services and Conservative Central Office being fully in the picture and still willing to make use of the fake item. The affair of the Zinoviev Letter was a squalid one from which no one involved emerged with any credit. Its impact at the time may not have been enormous, and probably it only changed the voting intention of a small number of voters. It was, after all, the Liberals rather than Labour who lost so much public support on polling day. But it showed that Labour's enemies were prepared to go to extraordinary lengths to smear the party's respectability, and that Labour was highly vulnerable to the allegation that it was tainted by its association with outside forces.

The outcome of the election confirmed that Labour – rather than the Liberals – was by then the second main party in the state. Although it lost 40 seats, it still won 151, and increased its share of the vote by 2.5 per cent to 33 per cent; the Liberals dropped from 158 to 42 seats, and won only 17.6 per cent of the total vote. The Conservatives romped home, with wins in 419 constituencies, and Baldwin became Prime Minister for the second time.

ASSESSMENT OF MACDONALD'S FIRST ADMINISTRATION

Although the experiment of a Labour government had only lasted for ten months, this was longer than many people had anticipated. On his defeat in the House in October, MacDonald – modestly but justly – claimed that ministers 'had shown that they have the capacity to govern in an equal degree with the other parties', and that they had 'left the international situation in a more favourable position than that which they inherited'.

Indeed, the government had not done badly. Despite its inglorious end, the government had some achievements to its credit. Abroad, it had effected an improvement in relations with France, Germany and Russia. At home, there were useful contributions in the areas of housing and education. In the eyes of its defenders, ministers had above all demonstrated their responsibility, and proved that Labour had displaced the Liberals as the only viable alternative to right-wing rule.

Unremarkable but not ineffective, the administration was at least comparable in its achievements to some other governments of the inter-war era. As for MacDonald, he emerged with enhanced esteem in the public eye. He was recognised as a credible, even rather impressive, international statesman. Yet the ministry over which he presided had not been a happy one. Dependent on the Liberals for support, it was vulnerable from the start to the unpredictable voting habits and intentions of the third party. Moreover, there were serious divisions at the top between the three main figures, MacDonald, Henderson and Snowden, and there was regular sniping from the left of the party both in and out of Parliament.

The government had performed creditably enough, and by the limited standards which MacDonald had set for it the objectives had been achieved. Yet there was inevitably much disappointment among Labour supporters with what had been achieved. Having attained power more quickly than might have been expected, many of them felt let down by their leaders. Above all, there had been little progress towards socialism. Whatever they understood by the term, they knew that they had not got it and there was little sign that MacDonald and his team were leading them towards the eventual fulfilment of their dream.

Socialists saw little sign of any new thinking, and some found themselves wondering in what respects a Labour government differed from a Conservative one. It seemed that it was really a matter of rulers presiding over the existing order more humanely. They would have liked to see a challenge to the existing order. This was the predicament for many people within the Labour Party. Should the party concentrate on seeking to replace the capitalist system by a socialist one, or should it concentrate on improving the life of the many via the routines and conventions of parliamentary politics? There were differing answers to the question. To the left, there were inherent flaws in the capitalist system and they saw the recurring unemployment of the 1920s and later the 1930s as a symptom of this breakdown. As an ideological party committed to a socialist system, exponents felt that they had the answer if only they could persuade leaders to abandon traditional attitudes and try their remedies. The fact was that unemployment was higher in 1925 than in 1924 after nearly a year of Labour government, and critics felt that MacDonald had not even tried to implement the policies advocated in *Labour and the New Social Order.*

DISILLUSION IN THE AFTERMATH OF DEFEAT

It was not surprising that MacDonald's leadership should be called into question when the inquest into Labour's defeat got underway. Many people within the Movement were dissatisfied with his performance, and they were not entirely critics from the left of the party. A biographer of Ernest Bevin, Francis Williams, makes it clear that his subject 'began to pull every string he could to get MacDonald dismissed from the leadership'. Much though he disliked them, he even sought and obtained backing from ILP members of the party, as well as from the parliamentary trade unionists.

Many supporters were disappointed and disillusioned with what had been achieved, yet after polling day there was no real challenge to his leadership nor to the performance of Snowden at the Treasury. Instead, there was sniping about the leader's personal qualities and fitness for his role. This dissatisfaction with MacDonald was widely expressed by prominent people in the Movement. Some cast doubts upon his adherence to party principle. For instance, Beatrice Webb wrote: 'I don't accuse him of treachery, for he never was a socialist'.

Others were sharply critical of MacDonald's leadership. Snowden let it be known that he considered MacDonald to have been inept as Prime Minister. He wrote to Fred Jowett and expressed the view of a number of members when he said that: 'I get no satisfaction from contemplating the increased Labour poll. That only makes it more painful. It is a proof of the great opportunities we have wantonly and recklessly thrown away by the most incompetent leadership which ever brought a Government to ruin'. It was not only that Snowden had never personally trusted the leader, it was the 'incapacity I never thought him capable of' which disturbed him most: 'He has thrown away the greatest opportunity which ever came to a party, and has landed us with five years of Tory Government. And his colossal conceit prevents him from being in the remotest measure conscious of what he has done. He is absolutely self-centred'. Snowden's wife caused an even bigger stir at the time by her observation, from which her husband never dissociated himself, that they had been 'the victims of the worst political leadership of modern times'.

Much of this animosity towards MacDonald was exhibited in the period 1924 to early 1925, and Beatrice Webb could detect in June of that year that the 'plain truth is that JRM has lost all his moral authority with the PLP as well as with the inner councils of the TU movement and his growing alienation from the ILP is only symbolic of a general "rotting" of his influence'.

He was bitterly attacked in the ILP paper, the *New Leader*, one critic advising the party openly to rid itself of him. Many other columnists and letter-writers felt that he had put up little fight in the election, and had made a serious error by allowing the Zinoviev Letter to be published. More than that, many of them noted that he had made a succession of weak speeches which had created bewilderment rather than clarity in the minds of the listeners.

There were attempts to get Henderson to stand against him, but when a delegation arrived he told them that 'to talk of swapping horses on the very morrow of defeat was disloyal and that he intended to stand firmly by MacDonald who in any event he regarded, despite all his faults, as the only man with the Parliamentary skill and public prestige to lead the Party back to recovery'. Beatrice Webb agreed, there was no one fit to replace him, and it was at the 1925 Conference that the turning point in MacDonald's fortunes came about. She noted that he had won 'brilliantly' and had totally 'reasserted his dominance'.

OPPOSITION 1924–9

The political initiative after the fall of the Labour government moved from the Parliamentary Party to the union leaders, some of whom were becoming increasingly restive. There were signs of increasing militancy in the General Council of the TUC, and the problems of the miners provoked a fierce controversy. They were threatened with lower pay and longer hours by the owners, and the TUC backed their struggle and called a general strike which started on 4 May 1926. There was almost a 100 per cent response, and as a result there were no national newspapers, and scarcely any buses, trams or trains on the first day. However, Baldwin's government had well-prepared plans to beat the strikers, and could make their views clearly known on radio. The contingency arrangements included the use of volunteer workers, and these often middle-class volunteers were keener to preserve established society than many trade unionists were to bring about a radical change. Some union leaders feared that if the strike went on too long then the ball would pass into the hands of the extremists. With such considerations in mind, the TUC suddenly surrendered on 12 May, and the general strike ended without there being any concessions to help the miners.

MacDonald was in a difficult position over this episode, for public criticism of the miners and those who embarked on the strike would only serve to isolate the moderate Parliamentary Party further from the industrial wing. Moreover, he recognised that the miners had been badly treated, and he could understand the sympathetic response of other union leaders to their predicament. Initially, he had participated in last-minute negotiations to seek a settlement and promised the miners that he was on their side. However, his support was emotional rather than tangible, and he privately disapproved of the use of the strike weapon which he felt was irrelevant to the position of the 'bankruptcy of the industry'.

Once the general strike began, MacDonald steered clear of it as best he could, for he saw that it was potentially damaging to the party's reputation. He attended General Council meetings, but as a silent observer rather than as an enthusiast for the action which had been undertaken. He wanted the dispute called off, and took the view that it was his mission to 'protect the political party from the same crowd rush of emotion which had brought the GC to this sorry pass'. Indeed, he went so far as to say that the episode was 'one of the most lamentable adventures in crowd self-leadership of our Labour history'.

In actual fact, he disapproved of industrial action as a political tool, and in an article in *Socialist Review* once the dispute was over he set out his views:

> The General Strike is a weapon that cannot be wielded for industrial purposes. It is clumsy and ineffectual . . . I hope that the result will be a thorough reconsideration of trade union tactics. If the wonderful unity in the strike . . . would be shown in politics, Labour could solve the mining and similar difficulties through the ballot box.

His whole approach caused some upset among union leaders. Bevin, as leader of the transport workers, was unimpressed and complained to the NEC of the Labour Party. Attempts were made at conciliation, but the gulf was becoming a serious one. Relations began to ease after the general strike was called off, especially when MacDonald became more involved in the early autumn in attempts to secure a settlement of the miners' grievances. By then there was little that could be done. Ministers had secured their victory, and the miners were starved back to work in November.

The cracks in the Movement between the political and industrial wings were papered over once the general strike ended, and the punitive Trade Disputes Act which followed the failure of industrial action further helped the healing process. This made large-scale sympathetic strikes illegal, and prohibited various forms of industrial action. By imposing the 'contracting-in' system for the unions' political levy, it also dealt a serious blow to Labour finances. There was nothing which the PLP could do to stop the onslaught, vindictive though it seemed.

MACDONALD'S DOMINANCE: GROWING OPPOSITION ON THE LEFT

Macdonald's dominance continued after the fall of the first Labour government, and at the 1925 Conference he spoke on three of the four days. Subsequently, there were left-wing protests at the ascendancy he had assumed in party affairs. George Lansbury exhibited frustration at the position achieved: 'The proceedings were managed and controlled from above. Individual delegates had very little chance ... From start to finish, MacDonald and Henderson dominated the delegates.' Yet a year later, the leader was even more prominent, and spoke on no less than 20 occasions. Indeed, by 1928 he was most emphatic that he would not allow the PLP under his leadership to be subject to outside domination or control. As he put it in a debate on policy towards India, he and his colleagues 'were not going to take their instructions from any outside body unless they agreed with them'. Most delegates had by now come to assume that the leader was to be treated with deference. One went so far as to express the hope that 'the Leader of the Parliamentary Party would be good enough to help them by reporting [on a particular point]', language not traditionally employed at a Labour gathering.

Yet MacDonald's mood and manner caused much hostility, and it was with the ILP that relations became particularly bitter. The ill-feeling was mutual. Some ILPers began to feel that he was leading the Movement towards destruction, and saw him as a failure as a leader of the working class. He felt that their approach was fractious and irresponsible, and that the behaviour of some members made Labour less effective in the House of Commons. He similarly often felt exasperated with the 'whirlpool' of 'class conscious trade unionists' around him. What was apparent was that by the late 1920s he was finding increasingly common ground with more reasonable Conservatives, hence Churchill's observation that Baldwin and MacDonald were more alike than any other two men who have held the office of prime minister.

The experience of government had provoked a major rethink in some parts of the Movement. Under Jimmy Maxton's chairmanship, the ILP had become hostile to MacDonald's approach. In *Socialism in Our Time*, produced in 1926, it urged the need for a planned economy, among other things. The statement emphasised the need for a 'living wage', a minimum for all which in its wake would help to revive the economy by promoting increased purchasing power. The dispute was partially about policy, but it was primarily one about the tactics to be adopted next time round.

Both the ILP and the Labour Party in general were agreed that Labour was committed to the strategy of winning power by democratic, parliamentary means. What the ILP demanded then and for the future was that the party should adopt proposals for a living wage, and that any future government (even in a minority) should base immediate policy upon them, deliberately inviting defeat in order to make a further appeal to the electorate.

More than two-thirds of the Parliamentary Party actually held a nominal membership of the ILP, and its behaviour was of importance. However, the language of Maxton and others in the ILP leadership was often uncompromising and they were not the men to sell their policy and approach to a PLP in which orthodox thinking was generally the order of the day. Neither MacDonald, Snowden or trade unionists were likely to be impressed.

At the 1927 Conference, the ILP made its attitude to MacDonald apparent, when it refused to renominate him to the treasurership, the post he had held since 1912. The gap was becoming unbridgeable, and the links of the ILP and Labour were placed under serious strain. MacDonald remained a member of the ILP, but it was ever more apparent that his conception of socialism and that of its members was very different. In 1928, the rival and official *Labour and the Nation* programme was adopted. The party thus accepted an essentially moderate document which was considerably less far-reaching than Webb's programme of ten years earlier, which it replaced. As Maxton

A 1929 poster suggests that MacDonald has the right qualities to run the country

warned the Conference, the way was assured for the next Labour government to 'do as it pleases' and again take the 'prudent' course.

In essence, the disagreement was still there between those who thought that Labour should opt for bold socialist measures which might lead to the government's downfall and provide the basis for an appeal to the country, and those who thought it was better to 'play safe' and opt for ameliorative reforms which might command the support of Parliament and show that Labour was fit to govern. It was largely a conflict between the claims of the socialists in the party and those whose main concern was to provide effective parliamentary representation for the working classes. Much antagonism sprang from a dispute over which of these aims was paramount. Intellectual socialists often felt that the party was little more than the political wing of the union movement; union leaders often felt that left-wing intellectuals were insufficiently understanding of the immediate needs of working people for a better standard of life.

There was never any doubt about what MacDonald felt. Whilst despairing of the unions and thinking of himself as a socialist, he was still an exponent of gradualism and 'realism'. For him, the publication of *Labour and the Nation* was something of a peak in his career, for it marked as he put it a recognition of the need for 'a synthesis between sound theory and evolutionary action'. Throughout the period of his leadership he had his way in spite of considerable opposition from sections of the parliamentary and extra-parliamentary party. In 1929, as an election loomed, the industrial and the political wings, the unions and the socialists, united once more to work for the return of a Labour government. For the first time in British history, Labour was about to win a majority (although not an absolute majority) in Parliament.

THE 1929 ELECTION

Baldwin called an election for late May 1929, and the general expectation was that his party would be returned to office. The three parties were all fielding more than 500 candidates, and it seemed likely that with a stronger Liberal presence the anti-Conservative vote would be split, making the outgoing government's chances all the more promising. Baldwin campaigned on the uninspiring slogan of 'Safety First', an indication that he represented stability and continuity. The Liberals offered a distinctive programme, based on an attempt to conquer unemployment via ambitious schemes of public works. Labour was sceptical about the soundness of Lloyd George's plans, and put its faith in longer-term measures to bring about industrial recovery. MacDonald stood down in Aberavon, for his constituents there were heavy in the demands made upon his time. They expected to see much of their elected representative, and he found that such a commitment left him insufficient time for his leadership role. He inherited Sidney Webb's constituency of Seaham in County Durham, where there was a vast Labour majority and the local association would be proud to be represented by an eminent figure and was less troubled about the frequency of the member's appearances in the area. He won by nearly 29 000 votes, and Labour was victorious nationally – even though because of a quirk in the electoral system it actually polled fewer votes than the Conservatives. With 288 seats, it was the largest party; it remained 20 short of an overall majority and would again require Liberal backing.

At this point, MacDonald's abilities and performance were at their zenith. He had survived continuous criticism and emerged with his leadership firmly intact. He had the authority which belongs to an ex-Prime Minister. Beatrice Webb wrote an assessment of him in her diary, in 1926, and in it she recognised 'his gifts as a political leader', including 'personal charm, diligence, self-control and a certain resourcefulness'. She knew that he stood head and shoulders above all other potential leaders, yet still there were reservations. Others within a very few years were to echo some of her thoughts:

> My general impression is that JRM feels himself to be the indispensable leader of a new political party which is bound to come into office within his lifetime – a correct forecast, I think. He is no longer intent on social reform – any indignation he ever had at the present distribution of wealth he has lost; his real and intimate life is associating with non-political aristocratic society, surrounded with the beauty and dignity which wealth can buy and social experience can direct. Ramsay MacDonald is not distinguished in intellect or character, and he has some very mean traits in his nature.

timeline	1922	election; Labour Party emerges as main party of alternative government
	1924	January: Labour assumes office for first time; Labour in office: modest measures to help unemployed, improvements to public housing and

in educational opportunity, handling of reparations and Ruhr invasion, support for League of Nations, Geneva Protocol, difficult relations with USSR

October: fall of Ministry over Campbell case; election on 31 October, followed by resignation in November; easy Tory victory

1924–9	leadership of Opposition
1926	General Strike
1928	official Labour programme put forward, *Labour and the Nation*
1929	election.

Points to consider

1) In what respects did MacDonald find working with his parliamentary colleagues frustrating?
2) What were the main difficulties in forming Labour's first administration?
3) Why was Labour unable or unwilling to effect a more radical programme in government?
4) 'Labour ... has made a mark upon the foreign policy of the country' (*The Observer*, August 1924). Was this assessment justified?
5) Why did Labour lose the 1924 election?
6) Why was the general strike a potential minefield for any Labour leader? How well did MacDonald cope with the problems it presented?
7) How effective was MacDonald as leader of the Opposition, 1924–9?

5

FROM LABOUR TO NATIONAL
LEADERSHIP, 1929–31

MacDonald's second Cabinet was broadly similar to the one which
served in 1924, and therefore predominantly right-wing in its
complexion. Haldane had died in 1928, but the other key figures were
still available for inclusion. MacDonald chose most of the same
personnel, but the allocation of posts was considerably different. He
relinquished the Foreign Office, and with some reluctance was
persuaded by Henderson that the job should go to him, rather than to
a more flexible personality. Snowden continued at the Exchequer,
Thomas was made Lord Privy Seal (and given a special responsibility for
tackling unemployment) and Clynes gained the Home Office. The
surprising omission, in view of his earlier success, was Wheatley who –
in MacDonald's view – was too clearly associated with the now
discredited ILP. There was one prominent left-winger in the Cabinet,
George Lansbury, but he was given a relatively minor responsibility as
Minister of Works, where it was felt that he could do little harm and not
be in a position to squander money.

A significant breakthrough was the appointment of the first woman
to Cabinet office, Margaret Bondfield becoming Minister of Labour.
Hers was not to prove a popular appointment either within the
department or within the PLP. Other choices were considered more
acceptable by party colleagues. In particular, some able politicians were
brought into the lower ranks, including Hugh Dalton and Oswald
Mosley. But the men who were to dominate the ministry were the same
ageing group as before – men whose willingness to innovate and
experiment had never been very apparent even in their younger days.

It was, as the Webbs noted, a 'government composed overwhelmingly of the Right section of the movement'. They analysed the membership and concluded that six members belonged to the old governing class, five (including MacDonald) to the lower middle class and six to the working class with two slightly outside. To the Webbs, the brains were to be found in the lower middle class, Sidney Webb (now Lord Passfield) among them, and the 'predominant element was Proletarian … manual or brain workers'.

If anything, the government's position looked more promising than in 1924, for this time Labour was the largest party. Although it needed Liberal support, the Liberals were in the mood to back innovative reforms. Moreover, such a Cabinet of moderates might enable the government to achieve broad backing beyond the Labour Party for any measures deemed to be necessary. There was much goodwill towards the new administration, and in recognition of the general atmosphere MacDonald used the King's Speech to appeal to all reasonable people for support. He speculated as to whether MPs might consider themselves 'more as a Council of State and less as arrayed regiments facing each other in battle'. He was prepared to consult widely on necessary changes, and the statement set out only modest and largely non-controversial goals in domestic policy. In foreign affairs the approach was different. MacDonald emphasised the importance of this area of policy, for he saw the combination of peace and prosperity as going hand-in-hand. Good international relations would provide the background in which trade could develop, and central to his concerns was a belief in the need to develop a better relationship with the United States, which had a key role in world commerce.

FOREIGN POLICY

In 1929, the inter-war phase of international goodwill was at its height, and there was a widespread willingness in Europe and elsewhere to compromise and reach understandings. The new government was more than willing to exploit this mood, and both MacDonald and Henderson believed strongly in the merit of seeking agreement with other nations.

MacDonald took a keen interest in overseas matters, and was particularly anxious to retain control over the issue of naval disarmament involving, as it did, relations with the American government. The Washington Naval Treaty of 1922 was due for renewal, and he tackled the subject soon after taking office. Almost immediately he ordered a cut in the ship-building programme, and a slowing-down on the construction of a new naval base in Singapore. He then visited the United States, where he was well-received and his presence generated much interest. Beatrice Webb wrote of his 'feat of endurance and . . . triumph in political activities', and the *Manchester Guardian* described his speeches in America as being of 'exceptional merit, both for form and matter, and, being nearly all extempore, were really a wonderful tour de force. Their tact, vigour, and manly diplomacy could scarcely be overpraised'.

Henderson also did much preparatory work on the subject of naval disarmament, but it was the Prime Minister who presided over the conference of five powers in London which was held in January 1930. British, Japanese and US representatives were able to reach agreement on a reduction of their forces, but the French and Italians could not settle their differences and they remained outside the main agreement although they were willing to accept the idea of a 'battleship holiday' until 1936. The London Naval Treaty thus agreed marked the end of the phase of post-war demilitarisation, for thereafter – as militarism was on the increase in the Far East and Europe – it was obvious that there was little scope for further progress towards international arms reductions and eventual disarmament. MacDonald's role was widely praised, and the normally unsympathetic *Daily Express* observed that 'to the principal actor of the piece – Mr Ramsay MacDonald – there can be nothing but the laurels'. Within the party, there was much approval for his work.

Much overseas policy was at this time concerned with the Empire, which as a result of the Statute of Westminster (1931) was increasingly to became known as the Commonwealth. MacDonald was particularly interested in the problems of India where the tide of nationalist feeling was growing and disorder rife. He was familiar with the subject, having visited India and written books on it. He personally supported the idea of dominion status for the Indians, whereby they would acquire self-government within the Empire. This was rather short of the independence which Gandhi, Nehru and others favoured. The Simon Report was published in June 1930, and it recommended responsible government in the provinces, an increase in the size of the electorate, and the summoning of talks on the best future form of central government. Unfortunately, it appeared at a time of mounting tension and civil disobedience, in which Gandhi and the two Nehrus, father and son, were put under arrest. Indeed, the scale of arrests of Congressional leaders and others involved in the disturbances caused many Labour supporters to be uneasy. One of them seized the mace during House of Commons proceedings as a way of halting its deliberations!

At a round table conference in November 1930, MacDonald presided and worked hard to extract concessions from the princes who had gathered. But the absence of Congressional leaders who had boycotted the meetings was a serious weakness in the deliberations, and MacDonald adjourned the proceedings whilst further consultations took place. By the time of the second Conference in the Autumn of 1931, for which MacDonald had worked so hard, Labour was already out of office.

Other issues were handled primarily by Henderson, who had long craved the Foreign Office. He is generally judged to have been an effective Foreign Secretary, although from MacDonald his efforts won only grudging recognition. He lacked the Prime Minister's glamour, and was sometimes criticised for his preoccupation with his party work at Transport House. But most Labour historians have been impressed by his performance, noting his skill in patient negotiation, his honesty and his willingness to think through the likely consequences of his endeavours. At the time, his conduct of policy was well received by moderate Conservatives, and his efforts received the enthusiastic endorsement of Labour and the Liberals. They praised him for his internationalism, his support of the League and his initiatives in disarmament.

One of his early moves was to arrange for a resumption of diplomatic relations with Russia. In *Labour and the Nation* and in the 1929 manifesto, there was a commitment to settle outstanding differences by negotiating a treaty and by measures to revive trade. Henderson realised that this would be a difficult area of policy, for there was little goodwill on either side. At home there was deep suspicion still of the Soviet Union and from Moscow there was a constant stream of abuse of the government and its personnel. Henderson saw little point, however, in trying to bring about more peaceful relations in Europe without including such a vast country whose exclusion from the world of international diplomacy would be a destabilising factor. Moreover, inasmuch as there was strain and disharmony, this was an indication of the need for a new attempt to make things better. The recognition given several years before of the USSR had never been withdrawn, only suspended, and he set out to allow the machinery of diplomacy to function again. Propaganda was a main obstacle, for Parliament would never ratify an agreement without some assurances that the regular abuse from Russian sources would be controlled. After initially unproductive talks there was eventually a breakthrough in the discussions, and for the first time an exchange of ambassadors between the two countries was organised. An Anglo-Soviet commercial treaty was also signed, but this time there was to be no loan.

Henderson took an active interest in promoting disarmament, and did much preparatory work for a world meeting on the subject. His efforts won him the presidency of the Disarmament Conference in 1931. He was also instrumental in bringing about a British signing of the Optional Clause of the Statute of the Permanent Court of International Justice, and as a result Britain was bound to submit disputes to arbitration as a means of resolving international disputes.

The tenor of Labour's approach was to work for an early settlement of remaining disputes. Both the Prime Minister and Foreign Secretary sincerely believed in conciliation, compromise and disarmament, and wanted to see the League of Nations act effectively. Henderson was a regular attender at international conferences, and his willingness to act – unhampered by an excessive preoccupation with national interest and pride – was helpful in easing the path of international negotiations.

However, even by 1930, the omens for European peace were already less favourable. Stresemann, the architect of the German policy of fulfilment of her international obligations, had died the year before, and the mood for reconciliation was on the wane. As overseas lending to Germany was cut off and unemployment grew in Germany with the intensification of the depression, the hopes of reconciliation did not survive. In this same year, Mussolini declared that 'right unaccompanied by might' was an 'empty word', and boasted that: 'Words are a very fine thing; but rifles, machine-guns, warships, aeroplanes, and cannon are still finer things.'

The economic storm-clouds were gathering and, as they did, so also did the willingness of European nations to devote their mind to the resolution of disputes begin to ebb away. Conciliation and arbitration were out of fashion.

DOMESTIC POLICY TO AUGUST 1931: THE PROBLEM OF UNEMPLOYMENT
—

The handling of foreign affairs can be viewed as competent and successful, but the same cannot be said about the government's domestic policy. Expectations for a programme of social improvement were seemingly confirmed by the content of the King's Speech, for it included references to an attack on unemployment, a reorganisation of the coal industry, a rationalisation of the iron and steel industries to enable them to compete in world markets, slum clearance and better housing. From the beginning, the government's legislative programme was to be damaged by opposition from the Liberals in the Lower House and by Conservatives in the Upper one.

There were modest changes. A Pensions Act extended existing arrangements to include widows between the ages of 55 and 70, a Housing Act provided subsidies for slum clearance, another was concerned with the provision of more and better rural housing, and a Town and Country Planning Act gave local authorities more power to control local and regional planning. Other reforms related to the rationalisation of the agricultural and coal industries, and Herbert Morrison devised an imaginative scheme for a London Passenger Transport Board – a plan eventually introduced in 1933.

Several efforts were less successful. A proposal to establish a consumers' council to act as a watchdog for members of the public ran into opposition from members of the other parties who disliked the element of compulsion involved and sensed a danger to private enterprise. Three bills on education were lost, and the Coal Mines Act was only passed in a heavily amended and much-compromised form. It established a Reorganisation Committee with some legal powers to encourage rationalisation, and reduced the working day to 7½ hours; the reduction failed to satisfy the miners, who had hoped for a seven-hour shift. A Trade Disputes Bill to reverse the 1927 law on 'contracting in' was withdrawn because Liberal amendments threatened to destroy its main characteristics. An early attempt to please the Liberals by producing a bill for a fairer electoral system, the 'Alternative Vote', was frustrated by the hostility of Conservative peers, and that plan also lapsed.

The programme was very limited in scope and the overall effects were such that improvements made went largely unnoticed. They seemed to be largely irrelevant to the major economic questions of the day. The central question in domestic policy was unemployment, which stubbornly continued to rise. All parties had made this the key issue in the 1929 election campaign, although it was only the Liberal Party which offered any bold or imaginative thinking by way of response to the worsening situation. It had made the running on the issue ever since the publication of Lloyd George's programme in 1928 (*Britain's Industrial Future*), and in the build-up to polling day Labour spokesmen sought to annex his ideas and suggest that they were more likely to be able to implement the measures needed.

The new government had little to offer the unemployed, only a continuation of the half-measures of its predecessor. The problem was not yet at its worst, and the number out of work was actually slightly down on the previous year. However, within a few months of the government's takeover, the Wall Street Crash had shattered the American financial scene, and within a short time the blizzard from America was adversely affecting investment and trade over much of the world.

It was Labour's misfortune to assume office just at the time when the structure of the post-war economy was beginning to crumble, and the Crash exposed the frailty of the recovery of the mid to late 1920s. In 1930, just when the numbers of the unemployed might have been expected to fall as winter passed into spring, they kept on rising and did so continuously throughout the rest of the year. Meanwhile, governmental palliatives were all concerned with the dole, an umbrella term for the various types of payment which could be made from the Unemployment Insurance Fund and other agencies. It had no economic policy of any kind to tackle what was admittedly a situation of unprecedented severity, one which was engulfing most of the advanced, industrial world.

The Cabinet could not agree on any other programme of action. It resorted to the establishment of a number of commissions and committees. Lord Macmillan was appointed to head a Committee of Enquiry into Finance and Industry in November 1929, for ministers realised that there were serious and interlinked questions on which advice was needed – the reduction of employment, the balancing of the budget and the maintenance of the external value of the pound. The brief was to examine the operation of the financial system and its impact on the wider economy.

As Chancellor, Snowden followed an orthodox Treasury line, and another of the impressive-sounding bodies, the Economic Advisory Council established in 1930 (comprising 15 members, industrialists, economists and others), provided no agreed alternative solution. Although the Council contained people of much eminence, the bold and imaginative thinkers were outnumbered by more orthodox City voices. The MacDonald government was always much influenced by the official Treasury view which echoed ideas current in London's financial circles. As the minister initially responsible, Thomas was assisted by a three-man committee, including the veteran socialist Lansbury, as a representative of the left, and the Chancellor of the Duchy of Lancaster, Sir Oswald Mosley, a recent convert to Labour from the ranks of the aristocracy. Thomas had little grasp of the topic, and any suggestions which he did make were usually opposed by the Chancellor.

Mosley was one Labour figure who called for a positive approach. He was irritated by the slow processes of government, and by the lack of enterprising and clear thinking exhibited by several of his colleagues. He had a plan for an expansionist economic policy, and this included incentives to encourage early retirement such as more generous pensions, protection of the home market via import restrictions, rationalisation of industries under public control and the greater use of credit to finance development – the whole package being designed to boost purchasing power and create an upward spiral in economic activity. In 1930, he produced a *Memorandum* which set out his ideas in detail, but after strong opposition from Snowden (still wedded to free trade) and others, it was eventually rejected by the Cabinet as too costly and impractical.

The 1930 Party Conference debated a resolution supporting his approach, and this was only narrowly lost following an impassioned speech by the author of the scheme. MacDonald defended government policy on that occasion by reminding his audience that the progress of

OSWALD PUSHES OFF.

Mr. MacDonald. "WHY ARE YOU LEAVING THE SHIP? IT ISN'T SINKING."
Sir Oswald Mosley. "NO; BUT IT WILL BE WHEN I'VE DONE WITH IT."

A Punch *cartoon (March 1931) shows Oswald Mosley, a gifted and rising
Labour politician, deserting the Labour cause*

socialism must be gradual and in stages. He suggested that they were
'moving, as it were, in a great eternal ocean of surge towards
righteousness, towards fair play, towards honesty'. Such rhetoric was of
little consolation to those out of work, and Mosley was unimpressed. He
quickly became disillusioned by the lack of vision of his colleagues, for
he felt that the party had a great opportunity to demonstrate that it
could offer an imaginative and bold programme to tackle the major

problem of the day. For Mosley, the defeat of his plans was too much to bear and when ministers shrank from the opportunity, he did not wish to stay around. In despair of the Labour Party he and four other Labour MPs founded a New Party, and by so doing brought about their expulsion. Mosley was to turn to a dangerous new theme, fascism, and this only served to discredit his broad approach. Public works and novel credit schemes were effectively ruled out thereafter.

MacDonald did take the opportunity of Mosley's departure to move Thomas from his post and took over responsibility for unemployment policy himself. He faced an immensely difficult task for which he was personally ill-equipped. He knew relatively little of economics and relied heavily on Snowden for advice. Little practical assistance came from the Economic Advisory Council established the year previously, for although it sometimes challenged the Chancellor's outlook its members, businessmen and economists, were never able to agree themselves on a coherent package. They met regularly with the Prime Minister, but nothing tangible emerged from their reviews. There were those who wanted to see a programme of planned expansion, in the belief that judicious increases in spending would increase the purchasing power of consumers who would then buy more. This approach, based on promoting an upward spiral of economic activity, was unacceptable to the industrialists, who stressed the need for balanced budgets and a policy of greater thrift and retrenchment. Even if there had been any agreement on a bold package of measures, the Council never had the institutional clout to combat the fiscal orthodoxy of the Treasury. The Chancellor and his officials stuck to the line that the public expenditure implications of various suggested proposals made them unrealistic, at a time of falling government revenue from taxes.

In the deteriorating situation, the unemployment problem came to overshadow everything else. Ministers received much advice, but the remedies offered were often contradictory and mutually incompatible. The Liberals continued to urge their programme of public works, involving a substantial increase in public expenditure. Many members of the Labour Party argued a similar case, with particular emphasis on the need to protect the unemployed; left-wingers in the party were especially critical of the alleged inadequacy of provision for those out of work. Conservatives pressed for protective tariffs to keep out foreign competition.

MacDonald was seeking a policy which might command broad consensus, given his lack of a parliamentary majority. He was prepared to consult widely and listen to discordant voices, whether they were those of Mosley or Lloyd George, but whenever they were examined by Treasury experts they were dismissed as impractical and costly. MacDonald personally distrusted what he called Snowden's 'hard dogmatism expressed in words & tones as hard as the ideas', but he was himself sceptical of any suggestion that an expansion of credit could cure unemployment. There was a fear among ministers that any scheme such as widespread public works which increased expenditure and therefore the budget deficit would only make it harder to maintain the exchange value of the pound.

The Prime Minister expressed interest in the idea of a revenue tariff in 1930, but he knew that such a policy would arouse the deep hostility of inveterate free traders such as Snowden, and therefore provoke serious disunity in the Cabinet. John Maynard Keynes, a Cambridge economist, put forward the idea of limited protection in the Macmillan Committee and in the Economic Advisory Council, but free traders in the administration were keen to argue that unless there was a move to full protection (which they opposed) then there would be little benefit.

In March 1931 the government set up the May Committee of five businessmen and two trade unionists to investigate Britain's financial plight and produce solutions. In the following months, events in Europe began to have an impact. The events which triggered the government's collapse began in the summer of 1931. The failure of the Credit Anstalt bank in Vienna caused a panic in international financial circles, and a run on gold in London where many short-term investments were held by overseas bankers. The situation temporarily eased with loans from Paris and New York, but any hope of a return to stability was shattered by the publication in late July of the May Report. As Skidelsky puts it: 'The appearance of such a document at this particular time converted what had in essence been a technical financial crisis into a crisis of confidence in the Government and in the country'.

THE CRISIS: AUGUST 1931

The Macmillan and May findings came out just as ministers were preparing to adjourn for the summer holiday. In mid-July, the Macmillan Report drew attention to Britain's balance of payments problem. For many years the export of manufactured goods had not matched the import of foodstuffs and other materials, but invisible trade such as earnings on banking and shipping had kept British trade in balance. Now it looked as though there was to be an imbalance, for invisible earnings had declined in the recession. Macmillan did not recommend an abandonment of the gold standard, which would have meant that the pound no longer had a fixed value in relation to other nations' currencies, because it was felt that such a policy would precipitate a general collapse of confidence. However, individual members such as Keynes pushed their ideas of a revenue tariff once again.

Discussion of the Report was soon overshadowed by the one which followed its publication two weeks later. The verdict of the May Committee, with its preponderance of City ideologues, was published on 30 July. It predicted a larger-than-anticipated budget deficit of £120 million, and argued that this could be met partially by selective tax increases (amounting to £24 million) but mainly by cuts in expenditure (£96 million). National Insurance was to be the main victim of the axe on spending, and this effectively involved a 20 per cent cut in unemployment benefit – the justification for this being that benefits had risen and prices fallen over the previous years. On the same basis, cuts in the salaries of civil servants and in service pay were urged. Keynes and some others in the Economic Advisory Committee urged the Prime Minister to reject the May findings. A Cabinet committee to discuss them was arranged for 25 August, and this comprised MacDonald, Snowden, Henderson, Thomas and William Graham (the President of the Board of Trade).

Whilst ministers holidayed, the situation worsened, and the Bank of England was struggling to defend the pound which was under serious attack. From Lossiemouth, MacDonald contacted Keynes to ascertain his views on the crisis, and received the advice that Britain might need to leave the gold standard. This was not the judgement of the overwhelming majority of the bankers, and they called for urgent action to cut expenditure and improve the trade balance. The Prime Minister and Chancellor returned to London, and on 11 August were advised by the Bank of England that they had only a fortnight in which to resolve the deficit for reserves were being used up and in danger of being exhausted.

An earlier-than-scheduled meeting of the key Cabinet committee was arranged for 12/13 August, at which Snowden confronted his colleagues with the likely scale of the budget deficit, £170 million in a full year. On the second day, after rejecting the Keynesian suggestion of devaluation with little if any consideration, discussion ranged over the balance to be achieved between expenditure cuts and increased taxes. Snowden pressed for a tax increase of £90 million and an expenditure saving of £99 million, the result being that the nation's finances would be in surplus once again. MacDonald had accepted the need to reduce expenditure for several months, and in pressing his case for substantial reductions his only concern – so he assured those around him – was to ensure that the package agreed was equitable. There was no ready agreement, and Henderson and Graham were uneasy about cuts of the scale envisaged, especially those in unemployment benefit. They were anxious that the potential for taxation increases should be fully explored before they debated the more politically contentious spending cuts. In their opposition to what was being proposed, they were limited by their own modest grasp of matters financial, and they could only argue from the point of view of troubled party members who were worried by the effects of what was being contemplated. They had no alternative programme to advance.

The outcome of the committee's deliberations was a package which would yield a small deficit of £2.5 million, and the proposals were due to go before a full Cabinet meeting scheduled for Wednesday 19 August. Although the Prime Minister and Chancellor thought they had secured agreement for the recommendations, the same two anxious critics had not committed themselves. This meant that there was already the probability of rebellion when the Cabinet met. On the 19th there was no problem over the principle that the budget needed to be balanced, and similarly there was unity on the level of taxation to be raised (although disagreement on the best means of distributing the increases). So too was the suggestion for expenditure cuts seemingly accepted (Snowden was asking for 10 per cent rather than the 20 per cent which May had proposed), although there were those present who had not declared their hand. Margaret Bondfield was asked to examine alternatives to an increase in local rates which would result from the transfer of 'transitional benefits' from the Exchequer to local government. For Henderson, meanwhile, at this stage the discussion was a theoretical exercise, and the lack of overt opposition at the meeting did not mean that there was political unity on the way forward.

It was on the following day that the financial crisis actually became a much more serious political one, for it was on the 20th that the opposition parties were informed of the government's intentions and that ministers met with the party's National Executive Committee (NEC) and the TUC General Council. The Conservative and Liberal parties wanted to see more expenditure cuts rather than any increase in taxation; their target was unemployment benefit. From the other side of the political fence, the opposition in the Labour Movement was of a very different order. In an atmosphere of crisis, leading ministers consulted the TUC General Council and the NEC. MacDonald and Snowden informed those present of the dire situation with which ministers were faced. The NEC broadly supported the government's position. Delegates of the General Council of the TUC voiced their deep reservations and, after questions, they left to contemplate what they had been told. They also requested a second meeting later that day.

At a Cabinet session that same evening, when reports were received on the various meetings, it was becoming apparent that there was disarray within the administration. MacDonald ran into difficulty with his colleagues, for a sizeable and influential group would not support cuts in benefit for the unemployed. Agreement could not be reached on the Bondfield modifications, which included a plan to means-test transitional benefit, the payments made to unemployed people who had exhausted their rights under the insurance system.

The final meeting that day was the second one with the TUC, and on this occasion it was clear that there was intense opposition to any additional burdens being placed on the unemployed. Union spokesmen had different ideas on the measures necessary to balance the budget, a goal which they accepted as necessary. They urged different priorities, including a rescheduling of the war debt and additional capital taxation such as a special tax on fixed-issue securities. As for a revenue tariff, that would need the support of the TUC annual congress. Such a programme was unacceptable to the Chancellor and Prime Minister, for both concluded that it said nothing of relevance to the matter in hand. The meeting ended without any sign of agreement.

The General Council left those present in no doubt that it was against policies which might restore confidence at the expense of the working class. It would not back the measures proposed, prompting Sidney Webb to observe: 'The General Council are pigs. They won't agree to any cuts'. MacDonald believed that the delegation had made 'practically a declaration of war'. In his view, 'their observations did not touch [the] problem arising out of [the] immediate financial necessity'. He later recorded that Henderson, with his usual 'vanity and ignorance', had tried to claim the credit for any slight aspect in the discussion on which there was any accord, whilst distancing himself from any Cabinet proposal disliked by the TUC.

In his diary for 20 August, MacDonald asked himself the question, 'Are we to go on?' His despair was understandable, for he faced opposition both from the Liberal and Conservative parties as well as from the left. Yet by the next day he was determined to carry on the fight, for he took the view that to yield to TUC dissent would mean that in future 'we shall never be able to call our bodies or souls or intelligences our own'. He would not be thwarted, and would see the crisis through to the end of the story. In Cabinet, ministers rejected the union standpoint and agreed to support the course which the Prime Minister was advocating. However, they were faced with a Bank of England request for cuts greater than those previously discussed, in order that the projected deficit could be cut by half. This was not acceptable, and doubters among those gathered round the table in Downing Street hoped that they could get away with the absolute minimum necessary to appease the international banking community.

Later that afternoon, the Bank made clear its alarm, for its representatives pointed out that the reserves had almost disappeared and therefore new loans were necessary from Paris and New York. The opposition parties were notified of the dire situation on the same day, and when they returned from their consultations with party colleagues it was apparent that they could not back the government. They wanted to see Parliament recalled, and it seemed as though the administration would then be brought down and a new government formed under a different leader. At this stage, the idea of coalition was mooted, and Neville Chamberlain and Herbert Samuel (the acting Liberal leader) expressed their willingness to participate in a national government of some kind to handle the immediate crisis.

There was an imminent danger of financial collapse, and the political crisis had almost reached its peak. The Cabinet discussed the situation again on the 22nd, and MacDonald again urged additional expenditure savings amounting to £20 million. He urged that this must include a 10 per cent benefit cut, as well as other measures. Only Thomas and Snowden would go along with his proposals. The rest recognised that it was necessary to obtain the loans from foreign bankers and wanted MacDonald to find out whether cuts of the order he was suggesting would appease the other parties. If so they might reluctantly concede the wisdom of this further pruning of government spending.

The situation appeared to be more hopeful, and the next Cabinet meeting was fixed for the evening of the following day, Sunday. Much depended on the attitude of the bankers in New York, for if they were willing to advance further credits then the Conservatives and Liberals might feel able to acquiesce in government policy and not need to bring the administration down.

On Sunday 23rd, MacDonald saw the King, and outlined developments including the request for an American loan and the 10 per cent proposal. He made it clear that there was a real doubt as to whether Henderson and others would support the package, and that if they resigned then the government as a whole would do so as well. George V was disposed to back the incumbent Prime Minister, and was intent on seeking the support of the other parties for him. However, as he departed, MacDonald almost certainly assumed that he would shortly cease to be at the helm.

The King meanwhile sent for Baldwin and Samuel. It was the latter who made the suggestion that MacDonald should be maintained in office (if necessary with a reconstituted Labour Cabinet), supported by the other parties. Should this prove impossible to arrange, then the same Prime Minister should lead an all-party national government. The King knew that there was more chance of the second option succeeding than the first, and when he later saw Baldwin he obtained his agreement to serve in a coalition.

From then on, events acquired a momentum of their own. The Cabinet met that evening, and during its deliberations news came through that the American loan would be forthcoming, as long as the government could command support from the Bank of England, the

City and the other parties. MacDonald appealed for support, on the basis of the proposals he had previously put forward – including the 10 per cent cut. He made it clear that they were necessary in the national interest, even if they 'represented the negation of everything that the Labour Party stood for'. If there were significant resignations, then the Prime Minister made it clear that this would entail the resignation of the whole administration.

Some of his colleagues dug in their heels, and whilst 11 supported the cuts, nine opposed them. Broadly, the middle and upper-class ministers were disposed to back the 10 per cent cut, whereas those who were politically close to the TUC would not. Although MacDonald had won majority support, it was apparent that the government could not continue. He informed those present that he would see the King and request a conference of party leaders to be held the following morning. He collected everyone's resignation and went off to see the King, intending to resign at that point. He later recorded his own impression of that last Cabinet discussion:

> Consternation when I reported, but in the meantime news of terrible run on Bank. It was plain that I should be left almost alone with Snowden, Thomas, Sankey . . . [The others] chose the easy path of irresponsibility & leave the burden to others . . . I have once more experienced weak human nature.

The meeting broke up in some confusion, and several present had assumed that a Conservative–Liberal alliance was their likely replacement in office. MacDonald did tell the King that he would indeed resign, but it was arranged that there would be a meeting of the party leaders. That same evening, however, he received a personal appeal from the Sovereign to stay on and lead an all-party coalition. The idea of heading an all-party coalition was thus implanted in MacDonald's mind, though it still seemed as though he would relinquish the premiership.

He met the party leaders in Downing Street late in that same evening, and pledged himself to support a Conservative ministry, which had Liberal backing. It really seemed that he was intent on going, but overnight his resolve appears to have weakened. On the morning of the 24th, the Prime Minister told George V and the party leaders that he had the ministerial resignations in his pocket. The Sovereign again called upon MacDonald to remain at his post, and expressed his firm conviction that the three parties must come together and agree an arrangement. Baldwin and Samuel agreed to serve under MacDonald, and he agreed to lead a National Government which would tide the nation over the immediate crisis. This was to be a temporary expedient, and then the party battle could be resumed in time for a forthcoming election.

He returned to Downing Street for what was to be the final meeting of the Labour Cabinet. Members were informed that the King had asked certain individuals to govern, and that in the 'present emergency' there was no other course. Ministers were invited to offer their support, and it quickly became apparent that the majority would not. They were mostly astounded at what had happened, totally unprepared for the bombshell which had hit them. Herbert Morrison later recorded the sense of shock which ministers experienced:

> The Cabinet had been called and waited for the Prime Minister to return to No. 10 Downing Street. We were standing around the Cabinet Room, silent, each of us with our own thoughts. The big double doors which ensure absolute secrecy for Cabinet deliberations made it impossible for us to hear approaching footsteps, with the result that before we knew it the Prime Minister was in the room ... without preamble and hardly waiting for us to take our places, he calmly informed us that the King had invited him to form a National government, or a government of the personalities in which he was to be the Prime Minister. He brusquely told us that he had accepted His Majesty's commission.
>
> He added to his nonplussed colleagues that the National government would not last long. He said that they would confine themselves within quite a short period to rectification of the financial situation, to effecting the necessary economies, and then they would resign. We were all shocked and those of us who had no intention of going along with MacDonald felt we had been badly let down.

He offered little explanation, and there was no discussion. Those in attendance were too astounded to respond, and Sidney Webb later recorded that 'we uttered polite things, but accepted silently the accomplished fact'. Lord Sankey proposed a vote of thanks to MacDonald which was passed unanimously and, without further leave-taking, his colleagues left the room. Thomas, Snowden and Sankey supported him as he had predicted, and the others withdrew to decide on their tactics.

Later that day a 'council of war' (the term Hugh Dalton later used) was held to rally the bewildered opponents of the new administration, and to see that a united front was maintained by them all. Key Labour figures were present – Henderson, the party secretary, Lansbury, Walter Citrine and Bevin of the TUC. The government had collapsed, seemingly deserted by its leader. Within a few days, Henderson was once again elected leader, and within a month MacDonald and his small band of followers were to be officially branded as 'outcasts' and expelled from the party.

The second Labour government, like the first, was a short-lived and in many respects unhappy affair. It was not an especially poor administration relative to others in the period, and there were some successes in the area of foreign policy. But from the beginning, its minority status again led to compromises, frustration and defeat. More seriously than this, it was unprepared in the face of an appalling economic crisis, and it failed in its handling of this, the one really important issue with which it was faced. Moreover, this was the issue on which Labour – given its origins – might have been expected to show a special ability and concern. In mitigation, one can only stress the circumstances of 1929–31. The ministry took office at a singularly unfortunate time, and the Conservatives had been fortunate to leave the helm just before the storm broke.

OPPOSITION WITHIN THE LABOUR MOVEMENT

For genuine believers in the party, there had again been no signs of any socialist advance. The disintegration of the MacDonald government had shattered their hopes, and they found themselves doomed to a long and dispiriting period in opposition. MacDonald had expected too much of his party which had gone along with him for many years previously, whatever the individual doubts of many supporters. During his leadership between 1922 and 1931, the PLP and the unions had been supportive, but on this occasion he was demanding too much of their loyalty. His anticipation that he could carry half of the Labour

Party with him was not fulfilled, for apart from his two Cabinet colleagues and his son, Malcolm, only four others backed him. His personal support vanished almost overnight, and although he retained the position of Prime Minister, his former party associates were bitter in their denunciation. The bulk of the Cabinet and Parliamentary Party, the unions and members in the country came out in opposition to the National Government.

He paid the price for his neglect of domestic policies between 1929 and 1931, and in particular for his neglect of the party as a whole. The lack of contact between MacDonald and the rank-and-file had become a serious deficiency of his leadership, and in the grave circumstances of 1931 there were fewer reserves of goodwill upon which he could draw. The initial feelings of many of his new opponents were not so much bitter as disappointed and badly let down. They developed over the coming months into much deeper resentment, and the charges against MacDonald began to circulate more widely once (in spite of a promise to the contrary) he called an election in October 1931, to obtain a 'doctor's mandate'.

From Labour's point of view, MacDonald's actions in 1931 amounted to treachery. One MP released his pent-up feelings in a letter to a constituent. He referred to the National Government as having been 'formed at the instance of three of the greatest rascals and traitors the history of politics has ever known'. He went on to describe Thomas, Snowden and MacDonald as 'three of the greatest failures and humbugs that ever held office', before launching into his attack on the Prime Minister: 'I scarcely know how to speak of him and have long since found him out, with his indefiniteness, his airy gentility, his evasiveness and his complete lack of honesty . . . believe me, the formation of a National Government was not to save England, but simply to save himself'.

Clement Attlee was characteristically direct, and spoke of the events of August 1931 as 'the greatest political betrayal in our annals'. In the eyes of his critics, MacDonald's series of crimes was too much to forgive. He had supported cuts in unemployment pay, clung to office, and then led a campaign against his own party. Such a record was a formidable blow to the Labour Movement. It was widely asserted that – if he had not actually plotted the downfall of his administration – then he had been more than willing to exploit it as an opportunity to remain in office and ditch his colleagues.

The idea of a 'plot' developed within a few weeks of the formation of the new government. It was current in the election campaign, and Henderson came near to endorsing it in a speech he made in Burnley, on 13 October:

> The suddenness of the changeover was all the more remarkable in view of the fact that the possibility of a National Government had been in Mr MacDonald's mind for months, and had even been the subject of conversation without its having once been brought before any official meeting of the Labour Party.

Henderson was careful not to commit himself to an assertion that the Coalition had been actually planned in advance, but his remarks were ambiguous. MacDonald clearly saw them in this way, for the following day he felt it necessary to answer the 'charge': 'I find it is going about a good deal that the National Government was devised months ago. I am very sorry Mr Henderson stated that yesterday, because he must know it is not true. The simple truth is this: every one of you who followed the events of the last ten days of the Labour Government knows that if I can be blamed for anything it is for carrying on negotiations too long'. Again, the next day, he stressed that he had striven 'almost until the last sand in the glass had gone through to keep the Labour Government in office. That was my policy. My policy was not to go out but to remain in'.

Others also advanced the plot idea, but it was Sidney Webb's article in the *Political Quarterly* in early 1932 which most savagely laid into MacDonald's motives. He spoke of 'the whole unfolding within sixty-three days of a single drama, in all its development foreseen in advance, it is safe to say, only by the statesman who was at once its author, its producer, and its principal actor'. He went on to argue that 'we have reason to believe that JRM has had the idea of a National Govenment in his mind for some months at least. Underlying everything, there is the fact that he has come to dislike almost every section of the Labour Party, for one or other reason'. In this drama which the former Prime Minister had himself 'staged', it was evident that he had set out to smash the party which he had done so much to build, because of his disillusion with many of its members.

If he had indeed been planning the outcome for so long, it suggests that MacDonald was a remarkably gifted planner – but Webb concluded that he had displayed 'consummate art'. His wife wrote of MacDonald's

'supreme cunning', even allowing herself a 'sneaking admiration for
. . . the greatest and most artistic of careerists – a veritable genius'. But
whilst paying tribute to the ex-leader as a master-schemer, they both
failed to provide much real evidence that he had actually been able to
devise and execute a carefully-planned conspiracy. Webb refers only to
'various cryptic utterances . . . which the subsequent events have both
elucidated and recalled to memory'. Many others have accepted the
view of Malcolm MacDonald that right up to almost the end of
the crisis, his father 'was fighting as hard as he could to keep the
Administration in office', and even Webb accepted that there had been
several suggestions of a coalition government in the early months of
1931 'with which nobody can suppose that your father had any
connection, if indeed he had ever heard of some of them'. He again
wrote to the son accepting that the latter's account of the final Cabinet
meetings 'seems to me – as I recollect it – to have corresponded exactly
with what you report of his contemporary communications to you'. Yet
if he could admit that his own version was 'avowedly hypothetical', he
never withdrew the accusations which he had made.

It is impossible to say when MacDonald first considered the idea of a
national government as a means of resolving his acute dilemma, but
others have echoed Webb's charge that he had been thinking in those
terms for some time. Indeed, they suggest that by his behaviour he had
let it be known for some while that he was temperamentally disposed to
that kind of solution. Suddenly, he was confronted with a situation in
which the prospect of forsaking his own quarrelling colleagues and
joining with the Liberals and Conservatives must have seemed
tempting. Such talk of coalition was certainly in the air.

Bassett's account sets out to destroy the plot theory with a meticulous
account of the origins of its development, and establishes its lack of any
credible basis in reality. He also casts doubt upon the credentials of
some of those who gave it currency. Mowat was also dismissive of any
'evidence' presented, and he concludes that such as it was it only

> proves that a National Government of some sort had been
> discussed in high political circles for some time, and that
> MacDonald expected some crisis. With the chronic weakness of
> the Government's majority, speculation about its future was not
> unnatural . . . That he had decided upon it earlier, as opposed to

being vaguely predisposed towards it, cannot be proved. And for two reasons. First, supposing one can start a crisis (and MacDonald had not started this one), one cannot be sure how it will develop . . . Second, and more important, there seems to have been no anticipation of the solution actually followed, on the part of the Conservatives, until Sunday August 23 . . . There is no proof that MacDonald, or any of the others, had planned it so beforehand. But they were perhaps not very surprised at the outcome.

HOW THE NATIONAL GOVERNMENT CAME ABOUT: MACDONALD'S MOTIVES
———

When the Labour government collapsed, it might have been expected that the obvious outcome would have been an administration led by Baldwin who was, after all, the leader of the second largest party. However, the King persuaded MacDonald to continue as premier, at the head of a national government, and Baldwin and Samuel were ready to accept such a solution.

Comment has sometimes been made on the Monarch's role in the events, for there was little doubt that he was personally disposed to such an outcome. He liked the idea of politicians sinking their differences, and his overriding concern was with national unity which he thought that coalition could help to promote. Morrison, in his *Autobiography*, having suggested that the 'natural course' would have been for George to have summoned Baldwin to form an administration with Liberal backing, concluded his assessment of the situation by observing that: 'I have no doubt that the King was perfectly aware of his direct responsibility and felt that the Throne should at a time of such crisis play a more direct role than was normal in easier times'.

Of course, the key ingredient in the crisis was the intractable financial situation, but two other factors were the state of the party system and the personalities involved. In the late 1920s, Labour was replacing the Liberals as the main alternative to the Conservatives, but the older party still had enough support to deny Labour an overall majority. In addition, the two largest parties were faced with internal division, Baldwin suffering from the deep hostility of some influential Tories after his electoral failure in 1929, and MacDonald having a dissident left-wing which disliked the orthodoxies of government policy. With this disruption to the normal smooth operation of the two-party system, there was sporadic talk on all sides of a cessation of party hostility in the late 1920s and early 1930s. In the press, too, there was speculation about the merits of coalition, and in December 1930, with remarkable prescience, a Low cartoon had actually depicted MacDonald at the Cabinet table, with Baldwin sitting nearby. The caption read: 'The unemployment question having produced a crisis, Mr MacDonald forms a National Government'.

Moreover, the principal characters involved in the crisis were all persons sympathetically disposed to a coalition. As we have seen, the King was receptive to the idea, and the other two men were willing to follow the suggestion which Samuel had originally put before him. Baldwin admired MacDonald and in many ways was a kindred spirit. For some time before, he had considered an all-party administration, but had felt that it was not viable. Tariffs were likely to prove a thorny issue, and he felt that anyway the majority of his party 'would not stand it for a moment'. He was not personally inclined to coalition, having led the Conservative withdrawal from the Lloyd George one in 1922.

But although he did not expect a national government to emerge and anticipated that he would take over as Prime Minister, when the King's attitude was made clear Baldwin could see some advantages in taking office under MacDonald's leadership. He would be seen as 'doing the patriotic thing' by having agreed to serve, and as Prime Minister the Labour man would bear the brunt of the unpopularity involved in any measures needed to save the immediate situation. At a purely party level, if MacDonald did stay on, this would be damaging to unity in the Labour Party, and enhance Conservative prospects at a forthcoming election.

There was, then, in August 1931 a conjunction of circumstances which made a national government seem not only feasible, but actually desirable. Such a government tends to be a strong possibility at a time of national emergency when drastic surgery is required. It is the more likely when there is a minority administration already in existence, and the action being contemplated is of a type repugnant to its own supporters. Not surprisingly, there were in 1930-1 politicians who were ready to contemplate an all-party approach. This brings us more specifically to MacDonald's personal position.

MacDonald's Attitude to the Crisis of August 1931

Various explanations have been given for his reaction to the 1931 crisis. Pelling allows him an 'honesty of purpose', and argues that – lacking much understanding of finance himself and not mastering the nature and extent of the problems – he was excessively dependent on Snowden, his Chancellor, 'who was a broken reed. He [MacDonald] had devoted the previous two years to external affairs and matters of diplomacy, and had simply not kept in touch'. Others dwell on the personal factors involved, and in MacDonald's case they point to his ambition, his vanity, his sense of indispensability, his increasing detachment from the Labour Movement and his failure to grasp the sentiments of those within it, his preference for compromise and the subtle solution, and, in the case of those more charitably disposed, to his sense of duty.

His defenders emphasise his wish to put national considerations before party ones. They ask whether he could have abandoned the crisis, and by so doing left the unemployed to face the possibility of even more drastic measures from Baldwin and the Conservatives. MacDonald himself responded to the suggestion that he should have stayed on as leader of the Labour government and defied the international bankers. To have done so would have been reckless and irresponsible. As he wrote to a Labour MP in September 1931: 'If I had agreed to stay, [and] defied the bankers ... you would have been swept out of existence. Still I have always said that the rank and file have not . . . the same duty as the leaders'. The need to do his duty, to act as was necessary, at whatever cost – this was offered by the Prime Minister as his defence.

Reginald Bassett was an exponent of this viewpoint, and he portrayed MacDonald's behaviour as an attempt to preserve the reputation and standing of the party. If he had simply run away from the problem, then this would have seemed as if – when faced with a major issue – Labour was tacitly admitting that it had no answer. The electorate would have been given the impression that Labour was incapable of dealing with the big issues, and MacDonald was keenly aware that it must seem as though it was strong and courageous enough to confront the country's problems.

Bassett also makes the additional point that the Prime Minister was fully aware of the reception his approach would get from certain elements in the party. He pointed out that MacDonald called the up-and-coming young men such as Shinwell and Morrison together at the end of the final Cabinet meeting, and told them that he was effectively going into the political wilderness. He generously went out of his way to advise them that they should look to their careers and keep clear of a national government which many in the party would not understand or forgive.

If one concedes MacDonald's sincerity in adopting his chosen course of action, accepts that he was genuinely placing what he perceived to be the national need over party feeling and recognises that he believed that the cuts were necessary to secure the loan without which the country would be in ruin, nonetheless his handling of affairs is open to criticism. His failure to consult his colleagues more widely and to explain his thinking were highly damaging to his case, and partially explain why there was continuing bitterness towards him.

Why did he not make more effort to carry his party with him? We have already seen that there was much evidence in the late 1920s that MacDonald was becoming increasingly exasperated with the outlook and behaviour of some of his colleagues both inside and outside the PLP. In particular, relations with the ILP had sharply deteriorated, for he was of the opinion that the factiousness and irresponsibility of its members was having a detrimental effect on the standing of the Labour Party in the House. At the same time, he was also more and more out of touch with the trade unionists around him, for he felt that many of their attitudes, and in particular their class consciousness, were not what the country needed. With such a membership, there is some evidence that he even wondered if the party was fit to assume governmental responsibilities, a point which Hugh Dalton (one of his colleagues and a later exponent of the plot theory) took up in his autobiography, *Call Back Yesterday.* According to Dalton, MacDonald had first expressed such doubts as far back as 1908!

At the same time as MacDonald was becoming more doubtful about the qualities of many of his Labour colleagues, so he became increasingly well-disposed towards some Conservative members. Partly, this was connected with his relationship with Baldwin whom he admired. But there were others too who had won his respect. Back in 1925 he had observed that there were some younger Tories who were 'men of very great promise' . . . [Sooner or later] the partition between us and them will become so thin that they might as well break it down and come over to the Socialists' camp'. Baldwin interpreted this differently, and took the view that it was more a matter of the leadership in the Labour Party being more realistic than many of its followers: '... since the disastrous year of 1926, they have been trying to wean their followers from what they have taught them for a quarter of a century'. MacDonald was unable to so wean enough of them in 1931, and in those circumstances was prepared to make a break and establish the new National Government.

In his study, *A Prime Minister on Prime Ministers*, a later Labour occupant of the premiership and one who himself faced pressing financial crises and understood the demands on leadership that these entailed, was able to empathise with the predicament in which MacDonald found himself. Harold Wilson exonerates him of any complicity in a plot, and stresses that he never intended the outcome which came about. To the end, Wilson believed, MacDonald assumed that his party would follow him in taking the measures he thought to be necessary. He never imagined, until very late in the day, that a majority of the Cabinet would refuse to accept the terms which he and Snowden considered essential. Moreover, he really assumed that it would be possible to have a brief coalition to put through the painful measures, and that then the normality of party life could continue.

Could MacDonald have survived?

If the Wilson view is correct, then MacDonald miscalculated the situation badly. Perhaps he did not appreciate the depth of feeling in the Labour Movement as a whole, and really felt that he could carry its members with him. When he failed to do so and formed a national administration, he left many of them in a state of stunned disbelief. Yet it remains the case that, for all of the past doubts about his abilities and sincerity within the Labour Movement, for all of the suggestions of treachery and betrayal, the key figures made no immediate attempt to get rid of him until in Dalton's words, effectively he 'expelled himself' – firstly, by not turning up to a meeting of the Parliamentary Party on 28 August to provide some vindication of his performance, and then by going back on the promise that he would not lead the coalition into an election.

Back in 1924 Snowden had given his verdict that as Prime Minister MacDonald had been guilty of incompetence, and there were others in the party who shared such misgivings. It was obvious to many of them, as well as to MacDonald, that he and they were increasingly out of step. In August 1931 their worst fears were realised. Yet over the years few had attempted to rid themselves of him. Perhaps the reason is that provided by MacNeill Weir in his generally hostile biography of the Labour leader:

[MacDonald] had earned the admiration and devotion of the great body of the Labour Party by his oratorical ability, by his intellectual ascendancy, by his personal attractiveness, by his specialised aptitude for the job, by his debating skill, and by his knowledge of Parliamentary technique. Moreover, he had assisted at the birth of the Party, rendered it a hundred services and suffered with it in its many reverses. Above all, MacDonald's prestige had been built up by years of hard work, and the gratitude of the masses to their leaders [is] proverbial.

Beyond such gratitude is the fact that there was nobody else of remotely comparable quality. Some in and around the leadership may have had their doubts, but to the majority of members and supporters in the country MacDonald had looked and acted the part. Loyalty to leaders, even when there are obvious doubts about their capacity and/or sense of direction, is deeply ingrained in the Labour Movement. As Dalton put it: 'We [in the Labour Party] have a strong sense of social security near the top. To do a man out of his job, at that eminence, is against good followership [sic].'

Given such instincts of loyalty and the lack of other available talent, could MacDonald have continued as Labour leader and carried the bulk of the party into the National Government? David Kirkwood, in *My Life of Revolt*, reckoned that if MacDonald had turned up at the meeting on the 28 August, his attendance and defence of his behaviour might have swung the situation in his favour:

We all knew that national affairs were not going well. We had seen nations crash into chaos and had seen dictators rise to autocracy on the ruins. We were familiar with the idea of a non-party administration. Ramsay MacDonald had said on more than one occasion that he was willing to work along with any Party or any men, if by their combined efforts they could redeem the nation. So strong was the hold that Ramsay MacDonald had on the party in the House that, if he had come to the meeting, anyone who challenged him would probably have been howled down. The Clyde group were definitely antagonistic. They had lost faith in their leader. Others were opposed to coalition on principle. But they would have been swamped.

In Kirkwood's view, the case for the leader went almost by default, for the man who was sent to speak on his behalf, Lord Sankey, 'talked to [the PLP] like a benevolent old gentleman who carried peppermints in his jacket pocket to give to the poor workers'. Kirkwood's was not a common opinion, for many of those who did attend took the view that there was nothing that MacDonald could have said that would have convinced the majority of doubtful and in some cases hostile MPs. At that stage, events had probably gone too far for him to win their support, but things may have been different had he handled his colleagues differently in the few months leading up to the 1931 crisis.

He had made little effort to woo his fellow members, and sometimes seemed to be actively trying to rid himself of any association with them. Yet in the final vote on unemployment in the Cabinet, there were more with him than against him, and it may be that had he taken his colleagues in the party and particularly in the Cabinet into his confidence at an earlier stage he could have won their grudging backing if not their outright enthusiasm. Many would have been tempted to respond to the suggestion that the country faced a desperate economic situation and that it needed a broadly-based government to carry through the necessary remedial measures. Some would have been unreconciled, and certainly the ILP which was in open rebellion against him was unlikely to lessen its hostility. Others may have accepted the inevitability if not the desirability of the situation, and maintained their allegiance – recognising that he was a man of superior accomplishments to many of the likely alternatives.

But MacDonald was increasingly out of sympathy with his party, and parted with his colleagues with as much relief as with regret. He did so of his own volition. He was not immediately pushed, but came to the conclusion that it was not worth the effort to stay and fight.

timeline	1929	election victory; Wall Street Crash; appointment of Macmillan Enquiry on Finance and Industry
	1930	first round table conference on India; establishment of Economic Advisory Council; resignation of Mosley
	1931	establishment of May Committee; Report of Macmillan Enquiry; Report of May Committee; early August: attack on pound; run on reserves; 19th: Cabinet discussion on crisis – agreement on need to balance budget; 20th: opposition parties and TUC informed of gravity of crisis – Cabinet disagreement and lack of cooperation from TUC; 23rd: MacDonald sees King who sees Opposition leaders; seeming likelihood of Conservative administration; 24th: King asks MacDonald to head an all-party government; PM tells shocked Labour colleagues; 28th: MacDonald fails to turn up at meeting of PLP.

Points to consider

1) In what ways was the second MacDonald government in a stronger position than the first had been at the time of takeover?

2) What evidence is there from the second administration of Labour's ability to handle issues of foreign policy?

3) Why was Labour so unsuccessful in its handling of the issue of unemployment?

4) What were the main differences between the approach of MacDonald, Snowden and Mosley to the handling of financial and economic policy?

5) 'The TUC had made practically a declaration of war.' Is this a fair summary of the attitude of the union leadership to the question of cuts in August 1931?

6) Was MacDonald temperamentally disposed to party cooperation in August 1931?

7) Did MacDonald agree to lead a national government out of considerations of ambition, duty, fear or some other motive?

8) Why did Labour feel so bitterly let down by MacDonald's performance in August 1931?

9) 'MacDonald's actions in 1931 were really a logical continuation of the whole drift of his thinking over many years.' Discuss.

6

THE LAST PREMIERSHIP, AND AFTER

MacDonald and Baldwin worked together as a harmonious duumvirate. Having alternated in office in the previous decade, now they shared power, with the Labour man at the helm of an administration in which the Conservatives were the majority party. They had certain qualities in common, as Mowat put it, a talent 'for calming the passions and rubbing the sharp edges of awkward questions'. The National Government suited both men well.

MacDonald was effectively the head of a Conservative administration, and his powers of leadership were already declining. There was little hope that he could stamp a personal imprint on the politics and diplomacy of the era. If he had been younger, fitter or stronger, he may have had more success, but rather his health was fading and it was evident to those around him that he was ageing mentally as well as physically. He had nearly died in 1927 on a visit to the United States, but the real downturn in his health began in 1931. He was increasingly prone to insomnia and melancholia, and from 1932 he was diagnosed as suffering from glaucoma. An operation on his right eye kept him away from parliamentary business for several weeks. In many ways he was past his 'sell-by' date – his performances in the House sharply deteriorated, his speeches becoming ever more rambling, his thought-processes less crystal clear than once had been the case.

THE COMPOSITION OF THE GOVERNMENT

In the National Government, the three former Labour ministers other than MacDonald returned to their previous offices. Otherwise, the

Conservatives held four posts and the Liberals two, although in the ministry as a whole the Conservatives were by far the largest party, and the MacDonald faction was even outnumbered by the Liberals. Within the Cabinet, Baldwin took the non-departmental office of Lord President of the Council, for which he was admirably suited. He was a key figure in the administration for he commanded widespread personal support across the chamber. He was content to take a back seat and this arrangement worked, for his very presence was reassuring. A more active Conservative may have wanted a more obviously influential position, and to have taken initiatives which were unwelcome to coalition partners, whereas Baldwin was careful not to usurp prime ministerial authority. He provided support at the times when his guiding influence and experience were necessary.

MacDonald was well aware of the risks which he and other National Labour men had taken, and privately confided that they were going to their 'political deaths'. He still thought of himself as a Labour politician, although he was aware of the extent of his isolation as the attack on his behaviour in the August crisis gathered momentum. He hoped that it might be possible to reunite the Party once the immediate difficulties were over, and financial stability restored. Yet he never took the opportunity to address the Parliamentary Labour Party of which he was at that time still a member. He was unwilling to alter his plans to travel to Lossiemouth when the PLP met to consider its attitude to the new government. Probably he feared that he would carry few members with him, and that he would be heavily defeated.

When he was expelled from the Hampstead Labour Party and his Seaham agent notified him that in the eyes of the constituency association he should resign, the writing was on the wall. In the debate on the emergency package which ministers put forward, only 12 Labour MPs voted for the government, with five more abstaining. He despaired of the behaviour of his one-time colleagues, and thought that the party leadership had proved that Labour was unfit to preside over Britain's fortunes. Henderson, representing the party, saw it differently. Whilst he did not close the door on the possibility of MacDonald returning to the fold, he pointed out the gulf which separated the two sides: 'The Prime Minister appealed to the country. We appeal to that part of the country that we have tried to represent, and I hope that we will appeal on high, strong socialist grounds.'

This Labour poster for the 1931 election concentrates on what cuts meant for those least able to bear them

Snowden's budget served to widen the conflict further, but when Britain abandoned the gold standard the move had Labour support and for a brief time it seemed that there could be some possible reconciliation if ministers made some concessions on unemployment benefit. They were not offered, for the Conservatives in the administration were happy to see Labour in difficulty and looked forward to an election. MacDonald came to see one as inevitable.

Neither MacDonald nor Baldwin had been keen to hold an early election for within all parties there was internal dissension about the formation of the Coalition government, which by its nature implied a preference for sinking party differences. Neville Chamberlain and many other Conservatives took a contrary view, and – sensing an opportunity to smash socialism once and for all – they were keen to exploit Labour difficulties and divisions. It was Chamberlain who coined the phrase 'doctor's mandate', which meant obtaining the backing of the electorate for whatever measures were necessary to tackle the crisis; in other words, 'trust us'.

MacDonald was unsympathetic to an appeal to the country at this stage, and as the King's secretary noted in a memorandum to the King written in late September:

> He does not like the idea of smashing up the Labour Party at the head of a Conservative administration. He does not know how to run with the hares and hunt with the hounds. He has hopes of sitting tight now, and attracting a following of the Labour Party. This may take a long time.

Yet on the same day (28 September 1931), he was formally expelled from the Labour Party and there seemed little chance that such a 'following of the Labour Party' could be won over. As late as the 20th, he had argued that the objection to an election was justified: 'there is not even a theoretical justification for an election now'. But as the Conservatives intensified the demand, it was obvious that MacDonald was effectively their prisoner in a government that was still nominally under his control.

He had begun to contemplate an election in mid-September, and by the 26th his mind was made up. He hoped to strengthen the small National Labour group, although he was not optimistic that this would happen. Meanwhile, preparations were made, and Chamberlain drew up a draft manifesto which included a provision for a return to protection. MacDonald knew of the King's wish to see a sinking of party differences, and gained an agreement in Cabinet that the issue should be left open. His toned-down statement worked. The Liberals were to be kept in the Coalition on the basis that the Conservative campaign for the introduction of tariffs would not be made a key feature of the campaign. Candidates with the National label would seek a broad 'doctor's mandate' to deal with the financial situation in the way that was most appropriate. This might involve various expedients, tariffs included.

MacDonald had thus abandoned his pledge of the previous August, which assured doubters that the parties would 'resume their respective positions' once the emergency was over. Now he recognised the inevitable, and had to argue that the emergency still continued and that further cooperation was therefore necessary. As he told his Seaham

National Government posters in 1931 pointed to the failure of the 'socialist' solution. They illustrate how far MacDonald had moved from his earlier thinking – or the extent to which he was a 'prisoner of the Conservatives'

constituents, he needed a mandate 'to diagnose and to prescribe'. He felt awkward about campaigning alongside his new bedfellows, but even stronger were his feelings of contempt for those who had not backed him in his own party: 'How I despise the men who ran away. And how hard it is to have to appear to have deserted'.

National candidates differed on the tariff question, for whilst MacDonald wished 'to enquire into tariffs with an open mind', Snowden and the Liberals were very unenthusiastic whilst Baldwin and other Conservatives were 'convinced of the supreme value of the policy'. For now, the issues would be left for an impartial examination once the election was over. Agreement was more easily reached on the value of abuse of the Labour opposition. Speakers dwelt at length on the dangers of Labour's return, and in this situation MacDonald posed as the man who was willing to shoulder his responsibilities – as a truly national rather than a sectional leader. His role was central to the campaign, for Labour made him and his 'betrayal' the target of its attack.

Snowden did not stand for re-election, but in his broadcast in mid-October he was bitter in his denunciation of his former colleagues and dwelt on the dangers of 'Bolshevism run mad' which would 'plunge the country into irretrievable ruin'. MacDonald was less strident in his language, but he also played upon the voters' fears of what might happen. To illustrate the possible problems he displayed a handful of worthless marks from the German hyper-inflation of 1923 as a warning.

THE 1931 ELECTION

In the election held in October, there was a landslide victory for the government. It won 554 of the 615 seats, but it was the Conservatives who were the real victors for they gained more than 200, taking them to a total of 473. For the official Labour Party, the result was a catastrophe of terrible proportions, for they won only 46 seats, a huge loss on the 1929 performance. Moreover, their popular vote dropped by approximately 1.75 million, and several key figures in the leadership were defeated. Labour could make little coherent appeal, for it had no alternative policy to offer. By contrast, the National Government with members from all three parties could obviously seek the patriotic vote.

MacDonald's own National Labour contingent was pitiably small, considerably smaller even than the Liberals. He won in his own working-class seat of Seaham by a clear majority, but it was the votes of many Conservative supporters of the National Government which enabled him to defeat his Labour opponent

In the new administration, there were at first 11 Conservatives, five Liberals and four Labour men, although in the ministry as a whole the Conservative preponderance was even more marked than before. Sankey and Thomas retained their former positions, and Snowden, having gone to the House of Lords, became the Lord Privy Seal. The real force in the government was the new Chancellor of the Exchequer, Neville Chamberlain, who was largely responsible for the direction of domestic policy and came to dominate the Cabinet. He had much energy and a clear if narrow mind, but he lacked personal warmth, and his withering scorn and rasping voice won him few friends on the opposition side.

THE PERFORMANCE OF THE NATIONAL GOVERNMENT UNDER MACDONALD, 1931–5

In imperial affairs, the National Government was in many ways at its best. MacDonald and Baldwin were committed to the Statute of Westminster, and smoothed its passage through the House of Commons; it passed in 1931. This was the measure which finally recognised that the Dominions had grown to maturity, and were joined with Britain only by ties of sentiment and a common commitment to the Crown. They were granted complete independence, and were to all intents and purposes sovereign states, able to make their own laws.

The Baldwin–MacDonald partnership was at its most constructive in the handling of Indian affairs. MacDonald was personally very interested in the creation of a new constitution, and according to some authorities it may have been a factor in his willingness to continue in the National Government. The second round table conference began shortly after the new administration was formed, and this time the Congress Party joined the talks, in return for an end to its campaign of civil disobedience – despite vehement opposition from Churchill who spoke up for the Indian princes, and laboured the danger of bloodshed if the British raj were to be withdrawn. The talks were inconclusive and came to an end in December 1931.

Following a third round table conference, in late 1934 a bill was finally produced which provided for an all-India federation and greater political autonomy. By the terms of the Government of India Act in 1935, the most important issues remained in British hands via the Viceroy and his advisers, but many powers were handed over to the provincial governments and the Indian legislatures. In the most advanced provinces, control of the police was handed over as well.

In other areas the government turned to protection and introduced a tariff on goods from overseas. The time for free trade had passed in the economic depression of the early 1930s. Every country turned to quotas and controls of some variety, for none of them felt able to allow in foreign items at the expense of those produced at home. The consequences for employment were too serious, and in Britain there were at this time still 2.5 million out of work. For the Liberals in the administration (and for Snowden, a life-long free trader), protection presented a problem, for some of them could not entertain the idea of a general tariff. In Cabinet, Baldwin made it clear that the majority opinion was in favour of such an imposition, and that if those who believed in free trade resigned then the Conservatives could easily assume the reins of power and introduce tariffs themselves. MacDonald backed the majority position against the Liberals, but supported the compromise which was reached. The unusual constitutional doctrine of an 'agreement to differ' was put forward as a lifeline to those who found it difficult to bend to the wind. Any member of the Cabinet was free not only to speak but actually to vote against the collective view of the ministry to which he belonged.

The Conservatives were thus able at last to pursue the economic policy in which they had long believed. The time was ripe for an experiment on their terms, and free trade was about to be jettisoned. It had long been the prevailing orthodoxy, but among Conservatives there was a growing feeling that it was time to put forward a distinctive policy based upon protection. Chamberlain introduced the Import Duties Bill in February 1932. It was designed to place a minimum 10 per cent duty on most foreign goods, but exempted food, raw materials and Commonwealth products.

Baldwin and the Conservatives were hopeful that the Ottawa Conference in July 1932 would take them further along to the road of which Joseph Chamberlain had once dreamed, imperial unity. They had often alluded to it in their speeches but as yet it remained nothing more than rhetoric. Now that Britain had forsaken free trade, there was a real chance of bringing about mutual tariff reductions, and the place to begin was in Ottawa. MacDonald stayed at home, and Baldwin led the British delegation, though Chamberlain handled the more detailed work.

In addition to Britain, Australia, Canada, India, South Africa and New Zealand were represented at the Conference. They all now had fiscal autonomy since the passage of the Statute of Westminster. However, whilst they showed a notional interest in the idea of economic unity within the Empire, the Dominions were less enthusiastic about measures which would have actually promoted such a union. They offered very little to the British negotiators, but after protracted discussions which came near to collapse, a settlement was eventually reached by which imperial producers received free access to the British market for the bulk of their goods, and Britain promised to retain a tariff against non-Empire countries for ten years. The Dominions made some concessions to allow modest advantages to British exporters, but this was achieved only by erecting extra barriers against non-Empire foodstuffs. Overall the arrangements were more to the benefit of the Dominions. Ottawa was a disappointment and the best that could be claimed was that a foundation had been laid on which further amendments towards a more general liberalisation of trade could be based. For Baldwin, this was the key to a general revival of world trade.

MacDonald had reason to be troubled by the outcome, for he had already been warned that the committed free traders in the government were unlikely to be able to acquiesce in whatever arrangements were made. In September 1932, Snowden and the Liberals took their dislike of the Ottawa agreements to the point of resignation, for they felt that the deal represented a shattering blow to free trade. MacDonald was unhappy about their threat, not least because he felt that it threatened his own position. A Liberal secession would bring to an end 'the national effort in cooperation', and he would be 'regarded as a limpet in office'. Snowden recognised MacDonald's true motives, saying that, 'He was disturbed about his personal position . . . and kept on repeating "I do not know what to do"'. As MacDonald himself told the King, his position would be 'more and more degrading' if he was left surrounded by the

Conservatives. Nonetheless, despite such pleas, Snowden and the others left the administration and Snowden was soon to be attacking his recent colleagues with as much vitriol as he had once deployed against his old ones. With their departure the government became even more dominated by the Conservative Party. In reality, a MacDonald-led Conservative government was now in power, with support from a tiny band of National Liberals who felt able to forsake traditional Liberal attitudes and work with their allies after 1931.

MacDonald was only too aware that the Conservative preponderance in the ministry made life very difficult and embarrassing for him. He hoped that his presence might help to mitigate the impact of Tory rule, but on several issues he was becoming increasingly an isolated and ineffectual voice. In December 1932, he explained his position (and that of Thomas) in this way: 'There are ... two of us in the very curious position of being amongst the leaders of a party to which we do not belong and made responsible for a policy which we cannot control'. He found his position degrading and uncomfortable, and spoke of how 'the oppression of my companionship crushes out every other feeling'. In particular, he disliked his dependence on some of the local Tory bosses who helped to sustain the National Government in power, for they were 'an odd lot of colonels and sycophants, repulsively vulgar'. Not surprisingly, he considered resignation, but he persuaded himself that he must stay on out of a sense of duty; he claimed to be a necessary check on the activities of others in the Government. In reality, if he left office, he had nothing else to do, and work was a substitute for personal loneliness.

Much of the work in domestic policy in these years was carried out by Chamberlain, whose policies involved help for 'special areas', those industrial regions hardest hit by unemployment in the declining industries. He was responsible for the Unemployment Act which sought to accept responsibility for looking after the unemployed and to establish a minimum standard of living for them and their families. The idea of means-testing (for those on transitional benefit) had been introduced in 1931, and Chamberlain included it in his new measure. There was much opposition among the working classes to this provision of the Act, by which a family's assets were assessed as a basis for calculating how much relief it should receive.

Housing was also tackled and the Rent Act was designed to end rent control in the private sector to encourage landlords to make more accommodation available. The building programme also favoured the private market, boosted as it was by a policy of low interest rates. A housing boom got underway, with expansion proceeding at twice the rate of development in other industries. Such progress was helpful not only in tackling the problem of living conditions, it also helped to boost overall consumer demand.

The revival at home owed something to measures with which a former Labour Prime Minister was unlikely to feel at ease. He disliked some of the government's policies, but was unable to restrain them. He noted in January 1933 that there was 'no vision of the general situation & only concern to keep Govt out of practically everything. Deserted by Labour and Liberal parties, National Govt. inevitably tends to fundamental Toryism'. Unemployment did gradually begin to fall in some areas, but it was still high and he could do little to make the suffering more bearable. Hunger marches occurred in the early to mid 1930s, and because they were often associated with communist sponsors he felt unable to even meet the protesters.

FOREIGN POLICY 1931–5

The decade of the 1930s was one in which the great questions of peace and war assumed considerable significance. The causes of the Second World War are highly complex and much discussed by historians. The treatment of Germany in the Versailles Treaty of 1919, the failure of the League of Nations and the weakness of British foreign and defence policy under MacDonald, Baldwin and Chamberlain have all been targets for criticism, even if there is a recognition that the outbreak of hostilities in 1939 owed most to Germany's policy of aggression and expansion after Hitler came to power in 1933.

The era of MacDonald's premiership was to witness a deteriorating international situation, for which many politicians were ill-prepared. The glow of the Locarno settlement seemed a distant memory and new perils arose on the continent and elsewhere in which democracy was under attack and dictatorship on the increase. The Prime Minister retained his own interest in international affairs, and saw this as one area in which he could exert influence – the more so as he had a low view of the abilities of the Liberal Foreign Secretary, Lord Simon.

Early in its life, the National Government faced a challenging situation in foreign policy when the Japanese invaded Manchuria, then a part of the Chinese Empire, in 1931. The invasion has been viewed by many people as the first major blow to the League of Nations, but at the time there was little that Britain or any other country in the League could do about it. Britain lacked sufficient military strength in the Far East to thwart Japan, a fact which could be seen as an indication that disarmament had already gone too far. MacDonald on this occasion went along with the Foreign Office line, rather than support the Americans who wanted to issue a strong joint protest which would not have been matched by effective military action.

Europe was to be the main setting for British foreign policy in the 1930s, for it was from there that the major challenge to peace was to derive. In 1932, the Ten Year Rule which had prevented the armed forces from budgeting for war for a decade, was abandoned. However, 1932 did not seem an appropriate moment for rearmament, for a Disarmament Conference was about to begin, chaired by Arthur Henderson. Otherwise, MacDonald played an important role in finally resolving the lingering problem of reparations. He chaired a conference in June/July 1932 at Lausanne, and although he failed in his bid to have the series of scheduled payments cancelled he managed to achieve a settlement whereby in return for a German final payment, France and Britain committed themselves to close accord in international affairs and agreed that there would be no revision of the Versailles Treaty without their prior discussion.

Progress at the disarmament talks was soon undermined by the accession to power of Adolf Hitler in January 1933, for he was bent on achieving military equality for Germany, a policy which alarmed France and her eastern European allies who felt vulnerable to German military might. In October 1933, Germany left the talks, a decision which effectively killed the Conference though it lingered on into 1934. As Austin Morgan puts it: 'The era of peaceful reconstruction was at an end'. MacDonald feared the new Nazi regime, and much as he would have liked to continue the search for an end to European disputes via negotiation he reluctantly accepted that Britain was under-armed given the rise of German militarism.

In 1933, however, there was still much support for disarmament in Britain for revulsion at the horror of warfare remained alive in people's minds. Pacific sentiment abounded, and the Peace Society itself was strong and held regular meetings which were well-attended. Pacific sentiment was apparent in February 1933 in a celebrated debate at the Oxford Union. The motion 'This House will in no circumstances fight for its King and Country' was carried, for it appealed to those who were outright pacifists as well as to those who believed in the League of Nations. The East Fulham by-election of October 1933 provided a similar message. A Labour candidate fighting on a pacifist platform defeated a Conservative who advocated an increase in the strength of arms in air, sea and land. The victor secured a convincing win by 4840 votes in what had been a safe Conservative seat with a 14 521 majority.

The right-wing newspapers of Beaverbrook and Rothermere were sceptical of the value of the League of Nations and in response to their campaigning the League of Nations Union, a non-party group whose political support spanned pro-League Conservatives, many Liberals and the majority on the centre-right of the Labour Party, organised a massive survey of public opinion in May 1935. From the 11 million respondents to this 'Peace Ballot', it was evident that there was strong support for disarmament and for the League. Most responses to Question 5 backed economic sanctions if 'one nation insists on attacking another', but in the following question, which involved backing economic measures with military action, the result was a very considerable but slightly less overwhelming majority of 6.75 million for and under 2.5 million against.

The effect on the government was to encourage it to downplay the rearmament which increasingly looked necessary, and to stress support for the League, albeit with economic sanctions rather than military ones unless there was a direct threat to British interests. Those who opposed the conduct of foreign policy at this time tended to point out that nearly three-quarters of those who had answered Question 6 were in favour of using force, whereas those who defended it pointed to the not insignificant number who disagreed with such action.

In the same month as the Peace Ballot (May 1935) it was agreed that Baldwin should take over as Prime Minister from Ramsay MacDonald. The world had become a dangerous place, and there was a need to take measures to counter the threat to stability that a rearming Germany might pose. In a situation of supreme irony, one of the last events of

MacDonald's era was the publication in March 1935 of a White Paper, *Statement Relating to Defence*. Although much of the brief document was a justification of past policy, including support for the League of Nations, collective security and the search for a reduction in arms, it recognised that the government could 'no longer close its eyes to the fact that adequate defences are still required'. The paper bore MacDonald's initials, JRM, so that one of his last tasks in office was to prepare the country for rearmament, a reversal of the whole tenor of his approach during the greater part of his life.

ASSESSMENT OF THE NATIONAL GOVERNMENT, 1931–5

The performance of the National Government has been viewed very differently by post-war historians. If its name implied an all-party administration, its character – as we have seen – was markedly pro-Conservative, especially after 1932, and so any judgement is to a large extent a verdict on the Conservative Party. But MacDonald was in the early years the Prime Minister, and so he must bear much of the ultimate responsibility for what was done and left undone. Left-wing historians point to the long queues of the unemployed seeking their dole payment, to the horrors of means-testing and to the failures of rearmament. More sympathetic writers have stressed the fact that the government led Britain out of the slump, effected a major tariff revision, began rearmament against Labour opposition, and made progress towards Indian self-government.

Neither MacDonald nor Baldwin had any clear insight into the nature of economic problems, and consequently neither had any new thinking to offer. They had no answer to unemployment, and the more energetic Chamberlain thought more in terms of palliatives than constructive measures. But after 1932, the very worst of unemployment was over, and things slowly began to improve, even if the overall performance concealed some appalling blackspots in particular areas. There seemed little to be done but wait on recovery, which would as the decade progressed be assisted by the rearmament programme.

In 1933 Britain began a recovery which reached its peak in 1937. Steady economic growth, rising real wages, new industries catering for the consumer and increased expenditure on social service were the outcome of this revival which was the more impressive given the slow recovery of world trade in general. There is less agreement on the role of the government in promoting this upward cycle. However, what can be said is that in a decade when other countries were turning to fascism and communism, Britain remained wedded to the democratic route. Its achievements may have been less dramatic than those of some authoritarian regimes, but MacDonald, Baldwin and their colleagues returned the country to better times after the prolonged slump, and did so without sacrificing essential freedoms.

A NEW PRIME MINISTER: MACDONALD AND BALDWIN SWAP ROLES

Between 1932 and 1934 Baldwin acted as Lord Privy Seal on Snowden's resignation, and as MacDonald's failing powers were becoming more evident, he effectively took over the role of Leader of the House as well. The Prime Minister had talked of resignation ever since the events of August 1931, but it was not until early 1935 that he finally recognised that his premiership had outlived its usefulness. His prestige had slowly ebbed away over several years. Society had already labelled him as 'Ramshackle Mac', and in his last year he was an ineffectual Prime Minister. Indeed, for some time he had been incapable of sustaining public office, and his frailties had been at least partially concealed by the presence of Baldwin to stand in for him. His physical powers were markedly diminishing, and so was his mind. His speeches, always meandering rather than succinct – drifted into what Robert Rhodes James has called 'meaningless vapidity'. A rambling if vain old man, he was mocked in the House of Commons by some MPs who viewed his performances with increasing derision. He easily lost his way when speaking, and on one occasion the power of speech temporarily disappeared altogether, rather as had happened to Joseph Chamberlain in his later life – a comparison which MacDonald himself sometimes made.

MacDonald was clearly unfit to lead the government into the next election, and Baldwin was well aware of the decline in his faculties: 'Poor old Ramsay was a doughty fighter in his early days; it was tragic to see him in his closing days as PM, losing the thread of his speech and turning to ask a colleague why people were laughing'. Yet Baldwin made no attempt to edge him out of office, for even if he sometimes felt as though MacDonald was 'like an eiderdown wrapped round my head', there were ties of friendship between them and Baldwin had a sense of honour. In his view, MacDonald had sacrificed his party in 1931 by continuing as Prime Minister, and deserved to be treated with respect even when he was an object of pity.

MacDonald was held back from making the final decision partly from fear of what he might do with his time, but also because of his concern that the Tory right might be unleashed once he departed. He disliked the intense anti-socialism of its members, and wondered if it could be contained. But illness and political isolation had taken their toll, and on 5 June he took his last Cabinet meeting. Two days later, Baldwin replaced him with some relief, for he was aware that Ramsay had stayed around too long, and vowed that he would not make the same mistake. Yet his own final ministry was also to be undistinguished, and some felt that he too had stayed around for too long.

MacDonald was surprised at his replacement by Baldwin, for he had assumed for much of his premiership that they would both retire at the same time and that the Chancellor, Chamberlain, would take over. He was wrong and in the new government he and Baldwin changed places, MacDonald becoming Lord President. Of the old Labour contingent, only Thomas survived from the 1929 administration. Malcolm MacDonald entered the Cabinet for the first time, as Colonial Secretary at the youthful age of 34. The balance of the National Government was precariously preserved intact, but the elder MacDonald became increasingly marginalised.

The immediate task of the Baldwin government was to prepare for the forthcoming election, and he looked for an early ballot as a way of securing a mandate for rearmament. In the November election, the National Government again won a massive endorsement at the polls, winning an overall majority of 247 seats. Inevitably many constituencies were lost for the 1931 victory had been won under highly unusual circumstances. The election was a further vote of confidence in the Conservatives and against the alternative Labour Party. Neither did the National Labour representation fare any better, and both MacDonalds lost their seats.

Ramsay MacDonald was defeated by his earlier friend and comrade, Emmanuel Shinwell, who inflicted a humiliating defeat on the former

Prime Minister by a majority of 20 498 votes in the Labour stronghold
of Seaham which he had held since 1929. The level of unemployment,
the means test and a local strike all told against him, and many miners
had not forgiven him for 1931 and took the opportunity to inflict their
punishment. His return to Parliament was soon engineered by the
creation of a parliamentary vacancy so that he could remain in the
government. He was chosen to stand in one of the old Scottish
university constituencies, a type of seat he had once denounced. There
he remained as MP until Baldwin's retirement.

MacDonald played a minor role in Cabinet discussion, and his voice
counted for little when he did join in. He was wary of British policy towards
Abyssinia on which Mussolini had designs, and employed any remaining
influence to calm down fears about the Italian dictator. He was prepared
to see concessions made to the Italian government, his concern being to
see that Britain used its position as a 'pacifying agent' in Europe.

In 1935 MacDonald felt the death of King George V deeply, but he
never much cared for his successor, Edward VIII. He backed Baldwin
during the Abdication Crisis, but otherwise made little impact on public
affairs. In the last session of the Baldwin administration he was rarely
seen in the House and, unloved by many Conservatives, he was often
booed by the increased Labour membership when he did attend. He
was not a significant member of the ministry, and his anxieties about
the conduct of policy towards Spain and the dictators were generally
kept to himself. In February 1937, he noted in his diary that: 'The hard
meaning of the European drift with Nazi-ism in the lead is not
understood by the Cabinet, but the appalling thing to me [is] that it is
democracy which I see to be breaking down'.

When the Chamberlain government was formed in May 1937,
Ramsay MacDonald appropriately bowed from the scene along with the
outgoing Prime Minister. He accepted no honour. Whereas Baldwin
was to have a ten-year retirement in which he was reviled as 'the man
who had betrayed his country', MacDonald had only a few months left.
He had long been seen as the man who betrayed his party.

Depressed about the state of national affairs and about his personal
health and circumstances, he was ill again in the early months of 1937.
He remained in the House after he left the Cabinet, and even began to
contemplate life as a Labour member and a socialist once again, but no
one was interested in his return. The last months of his life were bitter

and disappointing ones for him to endure. He saw himself as a slowly drowning man who 'sinks below surface & person becomes vaguer and dimmer & is at last lost'. He died of heart failure in November, whilst on a voyage to South America. Later in the month a funeral service took place in Westminster Abbey and his cremated ashes were taken to his own Lossiemouth for burial. The MacDonald era was over, and only a few of his personal friends and family associates lamented its passing beneath the waves.

timeline	1931	expelled from Labour Party; calls an election for October and seeks a doctor's mandate; invasion of Manchuria
	1932	return to Protection; Import Duties Bill and Ottawa Conference; Disarmament Conference
	1933	Hitler comes to power; Germany leaves disarmament talks
	1934	third round table conference on India
	1935	Government of India Act; MacDonald and Baldwin change places; MacDonald Lord President; election; MacDonald defeated at Seaham by Shinwell; re-elected for university seat
	1937	MacDonald and Baldwin both retire in May; MacDonald dies in November.

Points to consider

1) **Was MacDonald's expulsion from the Labour Party inevitable?**
2) **What evidence is there of his mental and physical decline in the years after 1931?**
3) **Why were MacDonald and Baldwin able to work together so successfully?**
4) **Did MacDonald contribute anything of special merit to the performance of the National Government after October 1931?**

7

A CONCLUDING ASSESSMENT

MacDonald and Baldwin were key characters in the inter-war years, and as we have seen they had certain qualities in common. There was indeed considerable mutual respect between them, and they achieved a personal rapport of a kind unusual among politicians of opposing parties. They shared a mutual dislike of Lloyd George – one of the more dynamic characters of the era – but there were other attitudes they shared. Both were men whose contribution to British politics was to minimise class antagonism and stress national unity rather than partisan and sectional distinctions. Indeed, between them they acted rather as a kind of national bromide, soothing the nation and keeping the temperature down. As far back as 1923, MacDonald could write of Baldwin that he was 'a Conservative, but an enlightened one . . . on foreign politics his views are as near as matters, the same as mine. Really a good type of cultured liberal Conservative'.

It has been fashionable to denigrate the politicians of that era and compare them unfavourably with men such as Lloyd George and Churchill who were for much of the time kept out of office. The reputations of both MacDonald and Baldwin suffered a marked decline soon after their death, for the impact of war made writers look back on the pre-war period and be dismissive of those who were partially responsible for Britain's condition in 1939. Any successes of the two men were largely forgotten. As Marquand wrote:

> Policies which had once been supported by large popular majorities now seemed explicable only on the supposition that their authors had been unusually weak or foolish . . . Few saw MacDonald as the most culpable of the pygmies, but few doubted that he was, so to speak, one of the most diminutive.

Yet neither man was without more positive qualities, and in both cases their attempts to play down differences and to bind the people together, their pursuit of moderate outcomes, and their commitment to democracy are worthy of commendation. The lack of strong leadership might seem to be a weakness, and both exhibited a lack of imaginative thinking in dealing with the great domestic issues of the time, unemployment and rearmament. This does not mean that their services can be readily dismissed.

Indeed, the whole 'pygmy' characterisation of the inter-war era is now much questioned. It was a fine phrase, and drew attention to a general point about the lack of giant leadership in the face of giant problems. But nearly a half century after it was first put forward, many might argue that the leaders of the intervening period have not been so remarkably talented either. Perhaps the truth is that democracies in peacetime do not necessarily throw up great leaders, and it even may be that the excitement and drama associated with such figures is not what is required by most people when there is no crisis or major controversy.

MACDONALD'S REPUTATION

Writing of MacDonald's life, Asa Briggs has noted the tendency of historians and others to deal with him not so much as a myth but as two myths:

> There seemed to be two MacDonalds, one the socialist pioneer, the other the Prime Minister of a – spurious – 'national government'. The drama like that of Henry IV, had two parts, although the sequence was different. Socialist historians tended to ignore or at least to underplay MacDonald Part 1; non-socialist historians were unimpressed by MacDonald Part 2, some of them dismissing him, as Churchill once did, as a 'boneless wonder'.

Here we have avoided the pitfall and dealt with all aspects of his life, but the comment itself draws attention to two other features of the writing on MacDonald. First, the fact that his career has been open to a number of interpretations, few of them very flattering until the more recent revisionist studies. No party feels particularly at ease with the memory of Labour's first Prime Minister. Second, the claim that he was a second-rate politician, the 'boneless wonder' of Churchillian legend.

Churchill's comments on his contemporaries were often less than flattering, but are memorable for their insight and humour – even if they seem overstated and unfair. In 1930, he had been impressed by MacDonald, and described him as 'urbane, cultured, incorruptible . . . willing to drive the car of Empire down every slope . . . so long as he can put on the brakes and be praised for his skill in applying them'. But the the observation quoted by Briggs above is a good example of the pungent genre, and was made following a government defeat during the second administration. Churchill recalled how, as a child, he had been taken to a fair at which one of the attractions was to be the Boneless Wonder. He had wanted to see this creature, but his nurse had refused. She had assured him that he could see the Wonder when he was older, but the time had never come. He had waited and waited in vain, but then – as he looked at the Front Bench in the House of Commons – he suddenly realised (pointing to the Prime Minister) that his eyes were resting on the Boneless Wonder. On another occasion, in 1935, when MacDonald was in serious decline, Churchill told his wife that: 'You cannot run the British Cabinet system without an effective Prime Minister. The wretched Ramsay is almost a mental case – he'd be far better off in a Home'.

Many in the Labour Party were similarly dismissive by then. They had previously distrusted him but clung to him because of his electoral appeal. Perhaps also, as Malcolm Muggeridge wrote in *The Thirties*, 'they felt that what he was going to do had to be done, and that he must do it, leaving them free to dissociate themselves'. Once their doubts had, in their view, been proven to be well-founded in August 1931, he was more or less a non-person in the Labour Party. References in its literature were often limited to a couple of paragraphs explaining how and where the party had gone off the tracks, derailed by his ultimately treacherous performance.

To many on the left, the impression even now remains an unflattering one, and he is often portrayed as a traitor. For their predecessors, it was often decidedly malevolent, for there was a feeling that the 1929–31 administration had somehow been cheated out of power, and that MacDonald had been the conscious or unconscious facilitator of the process. On the centre-right of the party, although his sincerity is questioned less, his judgement at the time of crisis is much doubted. Some aspects of his character – particularly ambition and vanity – are still mentioned.

Liberals and others who inhabit the political middle ground tend to be critical of most of the leading figures of the era. MacDonald is often depicted as having been woolly and incompetent, a man inadequate for the task which confronted him and particularly out of his depth in handling the crucial economic issues of the time. They feel that the more imaginative policies associated with Lloyd George and Keynes should have been implemented, rather in the way that Franklin Roosevelt pursued bold, expansionist policies to lift the United States out of the depression.

The political right has not sought to come to his rescue, for in the first place he features much less in the thinking of most Conservatives for they lack the emotional connections with him which are felt by socialists and those of their ilk. Many Tories had never much admired him or warmed to his personality. Although the party was the beneficiary of his actions in 1931 which inaugurated a prolonged period of largely Conservative rule, within a few years he was already seen as something of an encumbrance. From a later perspective, the 1930s was a decade which many post-war Conservatives wished to forget for the popular impression of dole queues, the means test and the failures of rearmament was not one which enhanced the party's reputation.

THE MAN AND HIS QUALITIES

In his 1956 Ford Lectures A. J. P. Taylor admitted that in the writing of his material he came to see MacDonald 'as a man whom preparation of these lectures made me rate more highly, to my surprise and even regret'. Again, writing of MacDonald's approach to matters of foreign policy in *The Trouble Makers*, he suggested that although the former Prime Minister 'was often regarded as an empty rhetorician', he was – despite his style of utterance – the only 'realist' among those who talked and wrote about foreign policy.

It is easy to read the past with hindsight, as did some of MacDonald's critics who put forward some variant of the 'plot theory'. On reflection, they decided that in the earlier part of MacDonald's career he displayed signs of the attitude and approach which in their view were put to such deadly use in 1931. Some even doubted whether there ever was a genuinely national crisis at all, and that he had simply abandoned them and deserted to the political enemy. As Mary Hamilton, in her biography of Henderson, put it: '[In their view] this was dirty, poisonous; he now proposed to head a Government composed of their bitter and lifelong political opponents'. That was not what most observers thought before then, and if there were misgivings about his personality, his social acquaintances and his easy acceptance of power, there was also a recognition before 1931 that he had many qualities which marked him out as a man vastly superior in intellect and parliamentary skill to any of his senior colleagues.

There were foibles in his personality, as there are with us all. His weaknesses and failings were often noted: a certain pretentiousness, a degree of pettiness in personal relations, a touch of vanity, and a fondness for duchesses which he himself conceded. There were alleged deficiencies more relevant to his role on the public stage – an inability to make up his mind and an occasional opaqueness and lack of clarity in his thought. Even when the thought was clear to himself, it often emerged in a way which others found more difficult to follow. In his writings on socialism, he often used terms in an obscure way, so that when he felt he was being straightforward and simplifying issues others found his ideas abstruse. In his book *The Socialist Movement* (1911), he gave an account of his ideas on evolutionary socialism, and described the onward-moving, backward-swinging pendulum of progress in this way:

> The state today is anarchistic. We have gone well through our epoch of exploitation by individuals and classes, and the diastole and systole of history goes on. Or, to use a more familiar simile, the pendulum swings backwards – but not along the path of its forward swing. It has moved onwards.

Because of such language, it was possible for his wilder and his more moderate supporters to interpret his outlook differently. To some of his audience, his speeches sounded soothingly moderate and reassuring, whilst others detected (and some hoped) that at heart he was something of an extremist who found it prudent to conceal his revolutionary ideas in generalised and emotive rhetoric. Those who came to the second conclusion misinterpreted what he had to say, for if the rhetoric was sometimes highly-charged his underlying thinking was usually safe and cautious, and he lacked any sense of urgency to bring about a profound change in the capitalist system.

If his thoughts did seem cloudy and imprecise, this was not without benefit. Ambiguity provided opportunities for adjustment and compromise, and his ability to manoeuvre in tight situations made him a good tactician. There were other appealing qualities which he possessed. He lacked the simple dogmas of some of his colleagues, and his fairmindedness, his belief in the basic decency and goodwill of many people, and his optimistic view of the future were admirable characteristics.

His style was one which was well-attuned to the mood of the post-war era. With rather melancholic eloquence, he chided the selfish individualism of a predatory world. He disapproved of the greed and self-interest inherent in the industrial system, and through his writings and his speeches suggested that there was a better way to live.

HIS CONTRIBUTION TO SOCIALIST THINKING AND THE DEVELOPMENT OF THE LABOUR PARTY

As an early socialist thinker and writer MacDonald had been very influential. In many respects he paved the way for the development of democratic socialism as we know it today, although those within the Labour movement might be reluctant to concede him his due place. Some, in view of the outcome of the 1931 crisis, would make no concessions at all to his important contribution. As late as the 1950s a Labour leader, Hugh Gaitskell, could write a study of recent *Socialist Thinkers* in which he omitted any reference to the first Labour Prime Minister – even though he mentioned a number of his contemporaries.

The utopian aspiration of the early Labour pioneers was to create an earthly socialist paradise for everyone. For MacDonald, socialism offered a vision of a new society where the self-development of each person was integrally related to the development of the community as a whole. Such solidarity was not only desirable but also possible. Cooperation could be the substitute for competition, and public service could replace the profit motive as the spur to endeavour. All could live in fellowship, and learn to identify their own private good with the common welfare. Fellowship would be the force that would turn the socialist dream into a reality.

He may have been an idealist and a thinker, but his writings were grounded in practical reality. Marquand has neatly summed up his position as that of an 'evolutionary utopian'. He wanted to remove the fear and want from people's lives, and give them a better deal in a more just and fair society. As a result of so doing, there would be less wickedness, self-interest and class consciousness, and a far greater preoccupation with the common good. This was an article of faith to him, but when it came to the means of arriving at this utopia, he was convinced that it must be – in the Fabian phrase – by reliance on 'the inevitability of gradualness'. Hence his remark, 'One step! One step enough for me! Ah yes, my friend, as long as it leads to the next step.' The hymn he sometimes quoted, *Lead Kindly Light*, contained a couplet which summarised his feelings:

Guide thou my feet, I do not ask to see
The distant scene, one step enough for me.

He knew that when dedicated socialists became embroiled in discussion of the details of the socialist vision then trouble could arise. In his view, it was better to concentrate on making discernible progress in stages, dealing with each immediate task but always working towards the better world of which he dreamed. His adoption of gradualist socialism greatly influenced the character of Labour in the twentieth century.

His work as a socialist orator, thinker and party organiser had made a remarkable contribution to the development of the Labour Party. In the early days, he was an inspiration to the Movement, and was far more creative in formulating its ideas and policies than many around him. Along with Hardie, another illegitimate Scotsman reared in very humble surroundings, he dominated the Labour Representation Committee and its successes were to a large extent achieved as a result of their contribution. He was an innovative and single-minded campaigner for the new party after the change of name in 1906, but in spite of his commitment to it he was willing to foster progressive alliances, as he did with the Liberals in 1914 – and was to do later by working with disenchanted Liberals and others in the Union of Democratic Control during the war, and bringing sympathetic Liberals into his governments a decade later.

Like Hardie, he was a man of principle in 1914, and made a brave and unfashionable stand against the war. In the 1920s, he was the dominant personality in British politics on the left. He emerged from the first Labour government with his reputation enhanced, with wider public recognition of his abilities and with an acceptance that he was a man of considerable stature in handling foreign affairs. By the end of the decade, he had secured a personal dominance over his followers. He had helped to turn Labour's often warring ranks into an effective political force, and he was at the height of his powers.

His achievement in uniting the Labour Party was no mean feat. Labour contained persons who derived from two discrete sources. There was the small minority of largely middle class, intellectual socialists, the real academics in the party, who were often uncompromising in their beliefs. Often, they were members of the ILP, the SDF or the Fabian Society. They were to be found in meetings, attending study groups and at summer schools, and for many years they had an influence out of proportion to their numbers. Such men were grounded in the theory of the Movement and tended to ask of any proposal whether it was sound socialism. They were sometimes less concerned as to whether it was sound policy or sound politics. On the other hand, there was the contrasting and much larger element of the trade unionists, men who had a background of toil in the mines, the factories and the railways, or other large industries. In 1914, it was largely the former group which made a stand against the war, and the second category who were willing to serve in the coalition.

Hardie and MacDonald straddled both worlds. Their backgrounds gave them an understanding of poverty and a sense of working-class consciousness, but they both became actively interested in socialist theory and wished to propagate the new ideas. Hardie was stronger on class solidarity, and MacDonald more disposed to write pamphlets and much better at organising fellow sympathisers. Neither an intellectual nor a union boss, MacDonald was a pragmatist and a realist, who – though he never could develop a close rapport with the unions – understood the importance of unity within the Movement and wanted to impart a sense of cohesion.

It was part of his genius as a leader that he was able to weld Labour's diverse components into an effective party. For that task he was particularly well-suited, and persons in either camp could recognise his personal and political assets. Not only was he personally an impressive performer, strikingly handsome, tall and leonine in his best years, and endowed with a seductive mode of expression. His other qualities were also indispensable for, as we have seen, the very imprecision and cloudiness of his thought could help to obscure differences of opinion in a smokescreen of comforting phrases. They enabled him, too, to become a resourceful parliamentary tactician, which neither Clynes nor Snowden was, and a skilful debater, difficult to trap. With such gifts, the leadership of the party fell naturally into his hands, and he kept the elements together in a state of relative harmony for much of the time; at his peak in the late 1920s most could have faith in him and recognise his transcending abilities.

As leader, out of an often discordant and grumbling set of supporters he was able to create and guide a party which was neither solely socialist nor entirely trade unionist, but rather a development of nineteenth century radicalism, and a worthy successor to Edwardian liberalism as the party of peace and progress.

For the secondary tasks of convincing the traditional ruling classes, the Establishment and the electorate that a Labour victory would be unthreatening to the British way of life, and at the same time persuading his followers of the need to compromise on inessentials which would ease their passage and help them gain acceptability, he was again particularly well-suited. Ceremonial occasions were a potential minefield, given the King's concern with formality and Labour's sensitivity and fear of ridicule from its supporters. MacDonald was able to insist that it was worth making some concessions over relatively harmless issues if thereby the King's understanding and help could be secured on matters which were more important. If this seemed to involve conforming with the values of the middle and upper classes, this did not matter and was a price well worth paying to secure the acceptance which would enable Labour to take and operate the reins of power.

It was his great achievement to create a situation in which the Labour Party was acceptable and strong enough to replace the Liberals as the natural alternative to Conservatism. Circumstances helped the process, particularly the impact of the war on the Liberal Party and the clash between Asquith and Lloyd George, but it was MacDonald who had done so much to turn the party into a credible rival to Baldwin and his followers. In *The Past Masters*, the former post-war Conservative Prime Minister, Harold Macmillan, who was a member of Parliament in the 1920s and 1930s, wrote a portrait of MacDonald. His opening remarks stress the effectiveness of the work achieved by his subject:

> Historians will regard the rise of the Labour Party in the first quarter of the twentieth century as the most dramatic change in the long history of party politics in England. Roundheads and Cavaliers, Whigs and Tories, Liberals and Conservatives . . . until 1914, the two-party system seemed unshaken and unshakeable. The Lib-Lab and Labour group members would be no different in their relationship with the Liberal Party than had been the old radicals . . . They would grumble, bring pressure to bear, bargain, occasionally blackmail; but in the main they would see to it that a Liberal Government remained in power or that a Liberal Opposition was not broken up. Yet in 1923 a Labour Government was formed, which although in a minority in the House of Commons was still a true Labour Government, independent both of Conservatives and Liberals.

That Labour would become the potential party of government if only in a minority situation was MacDonald's great achievement. He saw it as his task to convince the country that his party was responsible, fit to govern, and that its programme was attainable within the framework of the constitution. He had to demonstrate to his followers that social progress could best be achieved by working through the parliamentary process, and that the constitutional arrangements were not designed to prop up the system but could be utilised by any party which could command the support of the electorate. It is the measure of his contribution that ever since he took over as leader, the party has either been in government or been the official Opposition.

THE MACDONALD GOVERNMENTS

His governments were not particularly impressive, and even the first one disappointed the hopes of those who wanted to see a challenging and radical programme. Office imposed a severe test on the young party which found itself hampered by a variety of considerations – the suddenness of the summons, its inexperience of the routine of government, the absence of any rousing and easily identifiable issue and of majority support in the House. The lack of a majority was actually in some respects not inconvenient for MacDonald, for it provided him with an excuse for resisting the more extreme ideas of some Labour MPs. He was in the convenient position of never having to reveal how cautiously he would have introduced a socialist programme under different circumstances. As it was, most members of the party were happy to go along with his decision to assume office, and many of them reluctantly conceded that it was probably wise to demonstrate responsibility rather than to abandon office with a bang.

It was the second administration that went so badly wrong. The man who did so much to develop and nurture the party in its early days and see it through to maturity, was the man who by his actions in 1931 dealt it a devastating blow from which it took several years to recover. He was unlucky to preside over the nation's fortunes at a time when there were serious economic problems, and a particular one of high unemployment and a resulting deficit caused by heavy dole payments. The party had no answer to the situation, and he certainly could offer no remedies. As he said, 'On unemployment I have lifted the cup to my lips and found it empty'.

Labour too easily accepted the financial orthodoxies of the time such as free trade, the need to remain on the gold standard, and the need to balance the national finances. The second Labour government spent two weeks in struggling to produce a budget which would satisfy the wishes of international bankers. MacDonald was prepared to challenge his Cabinet colleagues to accept a package of tax increases and expenditure cuts including a 10 per cent reduction in unemployment benefit. When it was obvious that there was serious opposition from a minority, including Henderson, who opposed the cut and outside from the TUC, he was prepared to allow himself to be talked into heading a national government.

In the circumstances of 1931, he felt that he needed and did not get much support from his party. Thereafter he presided over what was in effect a Conservative government, and soon found himself fighting an election against the mass of his lifelong colleagues. Calling an election was not a course which he would have chosen, but by then such was the strength of his new associates and so great was the adverse reaction of his old ones, that he gritted his teeth and fought the contest as a coalition leader – thereby inflicting on his former party a defeat of shattering proportions. The new arrangements were not as temporary as he had hoped, and the rest of the decade was one of National Government but Conservative dominance. For four years MacDonald soldiered on, a rather pathetic figure who had slipped into premature dotage, a politically impotent old man who had little influence over the conduct of domestic policy and only made increasingly rare appearances at Westminster. It was easier to posture abroad where he could find an acceptance as a statesman that was denied him at home. Isolated and unhappy in what was 'nae his ain hoose', out of depth when confronted with the phenomenon of Hitler and the need for rearmament, worried about the government's drift to the right, he found the times called for measures which to him – in the light of his past attitudes and behaviour – were unpalatable.

It was probably cathartic for his old and traumatised political associates to invent the dreadful spectre of MacDonaldism, the image of a man whose personal failings led him into cohabitation with the other side. In their eyes, MacDonald had in his last years become almost indistinguishable from the Conservative enemy, and he was seen as someone who had betrayed the party, its political ideology and its traditional supporters – as well as his own socialist antecedents. Labour was bitter, and in the working-class industrial and mining areas, where the party had such a strong base of support, there were deep feelings that MacDonald was a traitor.

For years, he has had a special place in the demonology of the Movement, the man who betrayed the party and was instrumental in setting up the National Government, a mediocrity and a Judas seduced by the trappings of power. The charge of 'MacDonaldism' is still liable to be used against any Labour MP who allows himself to associate too closely with the traditional enemy, and many politicians have had cause to reflect upon it. Harold Wilson was Prime Minister at the time of the centenary of MacDonald's birth, and in his study of prime ministers he comments that in 1966 the son, Malcolm MacDonald, approached him 'with the greatest diffidence' when asking him to speak at the lunch arranged by the family to celebrate the occasion. Wilson added that he was told that it would be 'understood if any references to 1931 and later years were to be condemnatory'.

The tragedy of MacDonald is that of a man who in 1914 took a principled line and rejected the position adopted by the party leadership, yet who 17 years later clung to office and thus caused his party to reject him. The circumstances were different, and so was his judgement. In 1914, his alignment with bourgeois radicals and anti-war socialists was perhaps the high point of his career as a socialist man of principle. Whilst the vast majority of the trade-union dominated party found it all too easy to succumb to the pressures of wartime patriotism, his brave and defiant stand could only earn him much popular opprobrium.

Things eventually turned out well, of course, for at the close of the war that faction of the party (led by George Barnes) which stayed in the Lloyd George Cabinet did not long survive, whereas MacDonald was able to stage a comeback. Perhaps in 1931 he could have learnt a lesson from this, that his was a party which did not greatly care for those who placed other considerations (be they the national interest and/or personal advantage) above their commitment to fight for the Labour Party. In the eyes of his critics, the two motives were closely intertwined. It was notable that in putting country before party MacDonald was also advancing – or seeming to do so – his own personal interests. Coalition was good for him in that it enabled him to continue as Prime Minister at a time when all expected him to depart.

In party terms he made the wrong choice in 1931. He saw loyalties which overrode the claims of his colleagues and his parliamentary supporters, and claimed that he was acting out of a sense of duty. For him, the nature of the crisis and the reputation of the party demanded participation by Labour representatives in a coalition government. Henderson had reached the same conclusion in the First World War, and Attlee was to do so again in 1940. However, in circumstances of peace in 1931, the majority of his party and most of its leaders saw things differently. They believed that they should stand and if necessary fall together, and were unwilling to credit him with noble motives.

Harold Wilson, on the occasion in 1966 to which we have already referred, had to choose his words with some subtlety when suggesting that MacDonald might have genuinely believed that he was putting the national interests of country above and beyond those of party. For MacDonald, there was no real choice. As Kenneth Morgan has suggested, it is hard to imagine him doing any differently than 'obeying his monarch's request to form an all-party administration' in the light of his past record. Yet in so doing, it must not be forgotten that there were many in the country at the time who were grateful for his willingness to stay on and see the crisis through. Moreover, at the time the lines between economic radicals and economic conservatives were much less clearly drawn than they seem in retrospect. It is easy to overlook the fact that even someone now widely revered, John Maynard Keynes, then spoke with several voices. He was not consistent in his recommendations to ministers in the years after 1929.

To the end of his life MacDonald always claimed to be a socialist, and whatever exactly is meant by the term it was a sweeping claim. By most criteria, he had ceased to avow socialist principles back in the 1920s, although like many orators in the Labour Party he knew when it was prudent to clothe his speeches to a Labour audience in appropriate socialist rhetoric. Any pretence of socialism was abandoned in 1931, and thereafter he made little effort to return to the party whilst making occasional remarks that he still held to his old beliefs. In the words of Austin Morgan, 'MacDonald's socialism was as politically meaningless after 1931 as it had been practically rhetorical when he led Labour to become a party of government'.

MacDonald departed from this life largely unlamented, with the anger of those in whose service he had laboured for much of his life still resounding in his ears. Since then, his detractors have sought to present him as a rather shallow social climber, a politician of second rate intellect and irresolute character, desperately desirous of personal advancement and wholly without principle or loyalty. Such a picture does not in reality bear much resemblance to the man who with Baldwin so dominated the inter-war era. His early life, in particular, does not read like the career of a man solely or even largely concerned with the advancement of his personal prospects, and neither does the picture accord with what many of those who worked with him said at the time, whatever their later outpourings. As Austin Morgan points out, however much it became fashionable to attribute past misfortunes to MacDonald's leadership, it must be remembered that his parliamentary colleagues 'elected him twice to the leadership for indefinite periods'. There was a time when they recognised the spell of his personality, his debating prowess, and the extent of his parliamentary and organisational abilities.

The overall impression of his career is one of personal and political tragedy. MacDonald had much to offer British politics in the inter-war era, and there were many decent and honourable qualities which he possessed. He paid a heavy price for his decision to forsake the colleagues who had trusted him to chart the direction of Labour, and by so acting he undermined its prospects for more than a decade. Yet in any assessment it must be remembered that he was the man who led the party into office and became the first Labour Prime Minister. For that he deserves much credit.

In the view of many Labour activists through to the present day, Ramsay MacDonald emerges as a figure who was too conservative, too much of a political insider and too lacking in what Glasier once called 'the instinct of agitation'. If he had a sense of social injustice, it was less developed than was their own. Outside the party, there are perhaps those who if they knew more of his earlier record might be attracted to someone who – like Baldwin – never believed in the class-based outlook which was commonly held on both sides of the political and industrial divide. They might see in MacDonald a man who was a highly successful party leader in the early twentieth century, a fine public speaker, a supreme organiser, and a man with the rare gift of being able to appeal to the emotions as well as the intellect of the British people.

Points to consider

1) Was MacDonald really a spiritual heir to the Liberal tradition in British politics, rather than a convinced socialist?
2) What were his main achievements prior to the late 1920s? To what extent has his work on behalf of the Labour Party been underestimated, and why?
3) What were MacDonald's most important contributions to the process of political change in Britain between the wars?
4) 'MacDonald was always more concerned with the national rather than the party interest.' Is this true?
5) 'A man of principle', 'A cynical opportunist'. Which of the two descriptions is most appropriate as a summary of the career of MacDonald?
6) 'One of Britain's least-admired Prime Ministers.' Why does MacDonald have so few defenders today?
7) What is most admirable about MacDonald as a man and as a politician?

BIBLIOGRAPHY

There are several standard works covering the inter-war era. In particular, a useful analysis of the key figures and the problems they faced is provided by the Access to History study, *Britain: Domestic Politics, 1918–1939*, by Robert Pearce (Hodder & Stoughton, 1993). This incorporates the findings of recent research.

There are some histories of the Labour Party which are worth reading, either in part or in whole, for they are able to fill in the background of the party's development and of the different strands within the Labour Movement. Of these, the following are worthy of closer study: P. Adelman, *The Rise of the Labour Party, 1880–1945*, Longman, 1972; C. Brand, *The British Labour Party: A Short History*, Stanford University Press, 1965, H. Pelling, *A Short History of the Labour Party*, Macmillan, 1965.

Three more specialist volumes on Labour history are: R. Lyman, *The First Labour Government, 1924*, Chapman, 1957; R. McKibbin, *The Evolution of the Labour Party, 1910–24*, Oxford University Press, 1974; D. Tanner, *Political Change and the Labour Party, 1900–1918*, Cambridge University Press, 1990.

The background to the events of 1929–31, the depression and the formation of the National Government, are covered by two valuable books: R. Skidelsky, *Politicians and the Slump*, Macmillan, 1967; R. Bassett, *1931: Political Crisis*, Macmillan, 1958.

Beatrice Webb's *Diaries (1912–24 and 1924–31*, Longman, 1956), offer many insights into MacDonald's behaviour, although the reader must beware of her own antipathy to the man whose merits she recognised but whose leadership she found frustrating.

Finally, there are the studies of various Labour figures, especially MacDonald: K. Morgan, *Labour People*, Oxford University Press, 1987; D. Marquand, *Ramsay MacDonald*, Jonathan Cape, 1977; A. Morgan, *J. Ramsay MacDonald*, Manchester University Press, 1987.

INDEX